The Art Of Shouting Quietly

A Guide to Self-Promotion
for Introverts and
other Quiet Souls

Pete Mosley

Copyright © 2015 Pete Mosley
Published by:
PSB Design & Print Consultants Limited:
Registered Office 38 Salisbury Road, Worthing, West Sussex BN11 1RD
Registered Number 1613161 - VAT Registered Number 371185455

No part of this publication may be reproduced, stored in a retrieval system, or transmitted, in any form, or by any means, electronic, mechanical, photocopying, recording, or otherwise, without the prior consent of the publisher.

The publisher makes no representations or warranties with respect to the accuracy or completeness of the contents of this book and specifically disclaims any implied warranties of merchantability or fitness for a particular purpose. Neither the publisher nor author shall be liable for any loss of profit or any commercial damages.

ISBN 978-1-873847-02-2
First Edition
Cover Design: Sally Sheinman
Worksheet Design: Claire Duffy
Editor: Janet Currie
Proof Reader: Anne Currie
Designer/Typesetter: Keith Turner www.mooli.com

About Pete

Pete works with people who aspire to do or create extraordinary things.

Talks, Workshops and Webinars

He delivers talks and workshops on Confidence, Self-promotion and the Business of Creativity for corporate clients, universities and creative and cultural organisations. He has popped up on a wide number of platforms – from schools in the Bronx, New York to the wilds of rural Leicestershire; from the Victoria & Albert Museum to daytime TV and radio chatshows and keynotes for business networks through to his 'Cheeky Letters and Dream Lists' TED talk. He creates and presents e-courses, webinars and podcasts that are distributed globally.

One to One coaching

Over the years Pete's clients have included many business owners and entrepreneurs, CEO's, a vet, a Roman Catholic hermit, senior managers (corporate and academic), rock musicians, visual artists, writers and cultural leaders. All have wanted to make their mark on the world and be successful on their own terms. He has helped them overcome the very different blocks to progress that each has perceived to be in the way.

Background

Pete has been in business since 1984. He trained as a coach with Barefoot Coaching Ltd – the UK's premier coaching company – and has a Postgraduate Certificate in Business & Personal coaching from Chester University.

Website: www.petemosley.com
Twitter: @petemosley

Acknowledgements

My sincere thanks to:

Janet Currie – for pushing me through the pain barrier in pursuit of editorial excellence.

Sally Sheinman - who designed my beautiful cover: www.sallysheinman.co.uk

Claire Duffy - for the lovely illustrations, worksheets and incidentals: www.claireduffy.com

Anne Currie – proof reader extraordinaire, for making sure i's were dotted, t's were crossed, and that the odd lapses into non-standard English – i.e. Glaswegian, were kept to a minimum.

Ann Bates, ceramicist - for her insightful reading of the drafts and her ninja confidence tip: www.annbates.co.uk

Kim Morgan & Geoff Watts, coaches par excellence, for their ninja procrastination tip: www.thecoachscasebook.com

Iszi Lawrence, stand-up comedian, historian and podcaster, for her ninja tip on public speaking: www.zlistdeadlist.com

Contents:

Author Profile
Acknowledgments

Chapter 1: Introduction   5
Worksheet: The Confidence Audit   14
Chapter 2: On Quietness   17
Chapter 3: What moves you forward?   26
Worksheet: You and your values   42
Chapter 4: What holds you back?   46
Worksheet: Deciding Priorities   66
Chapter 5: Possibility   69
Worksheet: The Reverse Timeline   74
Chapter 6: What are you on the planet to do?   78
Worksheet: How BIG is your world?   84
Chapter 7: Embracing Risk   87
Worksheet: The Dream List   96
Chapter 8: Finding your platform   99
Chapter 9: Relationships and Networking   107
Exercise: Mapping out your expert profile   133
Chapter 10: Asking for help   135
Chapter 11: Preparing for action   147
Exercise: The Wheel of Self-promotion   153
Chapter 12: What Now?   156
Worksheet: The Future Timeline   158

1 The Art Of Shouting Quietly - Introduction.

I've always been a shy person. It took a huge effort to get to the point of talking to large live audiences, writing for a national magazine, and blogging and writing online for nationally and internationally significant organisations – not only in overcoming self-limiting beliefs, but also in overcoming the well-meaning critical stance of others – parents, siblings, peers and colleagues.

It's not just the people you know, either; there's a whole industry out there that is designed to make you feel inadequate – physically, emotionally and intellectually. That industry then relies on the insecurities it generates to sell you everything from get rich quick manuals to cosmetic surgery.

In truth, we are pretty much OK as we are, most of us. This book is designed to encourage, affirm and support the positive qualities that you already have and encourage you to do extraordinary things by building on your own natural resources.

My first book – Make Your Creativity Pay, was written for people who want to earn their living from the things they love to do – to believe in themselves enough to do so, and if necessary, overcome the doubters and obstacles in order to make the transition from working for others to creative self-employment.

Things really take off when the strength of your ideas and momentum of your thinking overcome the astonishing gravitational pull of resistance and procrastination. However, the very best ideas also tend to encounter the strongest resistance – from doubters, critics, misguided mentors and the risk averse. These things conspire to create a considerable threshold to get across.

This second book - The Art Of Shouting Quietly, is about helping the quiet souls, the shy and introverted – and extroverts too - to find the mindset, tools and techniques to carry their message across and get their ideas flying.

I've been a freelancer since 1984. Over the years I have worked with hundreds of self-employed people. I have spent thousands of hours in conversation with them – usually at their studios or place of work. Many are very successful on their own terms, and it's the things that all those successful people share in terms of confidence, making their mark on the world and the cultivation of success on their own terms that I want to share with you in this book.

One of the questions the book explores is the perennial problem of self-confidence. It's a mercurial quality at the best of times and one which ebbs and flows for everyone throughout their lives. It's not something that you get once and then have forever. You have it once, then it escapes you, and then it comes back seemingly in a different form. We all need to find our own 'brand' of confidence and employ it in ways that are unique to ourselves.

With solid foundations built beneath it, confidence becomes significantly harder to rock and easier to recover when it is shaken.

What are those foundations? What do I hope this book will encourage you to do?

- Systematically reinforce your belief in yourself.
- Understand your place in the world - and what you were put on the planet to do.
- Know what drives you forward and what holds you back – and how to keep these in balance.
- Be true to yourself and your values.
- Know that you have the power and freedom to shape your own sense of what is (and is not) possible.
- Have a strong sense of plan and purpose.
- Know that asking for help is not an admission of failure – far from it!

- Develop the skill of asking for help in a structured way and understanding that this is not a sign of weakness.
- Know how to show up and share your gift in a way that sits comfortably with your values and mindset.

Why this book?

My life's work is about helping people identify the things that hold them back – and to systematically engage with and overcome them. This book illustrates how this can be done – with insights into what the blocks actually are, how to take responsibility for them, and how to stop blaming others for your own lack of progress. Every reader, I hope, will find something in the content that they will relate strongly to in respect of the obstacles and challenges in their own life.

> **What matters most in life is to be yourself, not what other people think you should be.**

As a quiet person, I often find that I struggle to find the space and time to think clearly. The world seems to conspire to fill every available moment with distraction and clutter. There's so much going on that I zone out sometimes.

But instead of doing what's right for me - that is,

deliberately separating myself from the clutter and taking the time and space to literally or metaphorically 'get away from it all', I sometimes slip into a state akin to sleepwalking. It's as if I'm just trying to methodically wade my way through stuff in the hope of creating a clear spot somewhere.

From time to time I also find that what others experience as normal and desirable simply overwhelms me. Too much going on – not enough space – no escape.

The realisation that I was an introvert freed me from a huge pile of self-doubt. I had spent years thinking I was more than a little dysfunctional. There have been times in my life when I have felt totally ill at ease in the world. I have slipped away from events at lunchtime to eat my lunch in the car, sometimes never going back. I have been tongue-tied at dinner parties despite the fact that I'll happily talk in front of 200 people. I've wandered off on my own at festivals to avoid getting caught up in small talk. I'm sure folk have thought me rude and anti-social. I was just trying to stay sane and do the best I could.

This book is aimed at people who want to find their place in the world, boost their confidence, know their gift or contribution, get a clear sense of direction, overcome blocks and barriers (real or imagined), and find the most effective ways to connect with the people that matter.

It is designed to be easy to read but also to pose difficult questions; full of ideas and inspiration that will spur the reader to action, give them confidence in their ideas and the energy to move them forward.

In asking the difficult questions, I'm also hoping you can find it within yourself to answer them honestly. Honesty, self-knowledge, acceptance of boundaries and limitations - and the courage to challenge oneself and change - underpin The Art of Shouting Quietly.

I use the terms 'creative' and 'creativity' a lot throughout the book. I'd like to be really clear that my definition of creativity is very broad, and I'd encourage you to think that way too. If you have started or are considering starting a small business, you are by definition creative. If you are a change–maker or assist people with their physical or mental well-being, you are creative. All of these things require creative thought to bring them to fruition. So when I say 'creative people' – I mean you too!

How does the book work?

The book looks first at issues of confidence and explores the things that motivate us and hold us back. It then encourages you to think about the avenues of self-promotion that will fit best with your learning style and values. Finally it will help you determine what you need to do in order to find your voice and use it effectively to build the relationships you need in order to be successful. By the time you have finished reading the book you will have a clear plan of action.

All of the worksheets can be photocopied or created afresh so that you can use them as often as you want. I recommend you revisit some of the worksheets every six months or so.

You will find 'Action points' and 'Points to ponder' throughout the book. Make sure you make the time to think about these things as and when you can.

N.B. This book will encourage you to be brave and get out there. Prepare to explore your stretch zone!

Destinations

> 'We shall not cease from exploration
> And the end of all our exploring
> Will be to arrive where we started
> And know the place for the first time.'
>
> T.S.Eliot – Little Gidding

Start with the end in mind. The end will change. There will be lots of ends. Process – the making of progress, step by step, is cumulatively more important than any single goal.

Loose ends don't matter. It's not your responsibility to tie them all up. Especially other people's loose ends, or ends they have imagined for you. Maybe there are previously forbidden ends that you'd love to unravel right now.

Just make sure it's you that chooses which ends matter most to you at any given time.

When I trained as coach, one of the things we were taught was to "Stay with the not-knowing". Uncertainty may be uncomfortable, but being patient and watchful pays huge dividends. It's the trying to control stuff that'll stop you in your tracks.

Best wishes - Pete Mosley

Ninja Tip - Procrastination

We all procrastinate sometimes and, although procrastination has a bad name, there can be positive aspects to it. If we never procrastinated we might make rash decisions. Walking away from things may not necessarily be a bad thing—it may be evidence of ability to exercise discernment and to make decisions.

However, taken to excess, procrastination can lead to missed opportunities, missed deadlines and dissatisfaction for both the procrastinator and those who have to deal with them.

Sometimes we procrastinate because we haven't clarified the true benefit we might get from doing what we have been putting off. 'Stepping up' can help us to think about a purpose bigger than the immediate outcome.

Rather than simply stating 'I want to write a book', it is useful to 'step up' and identify the reason why achieving this goal would be valuable to you. The answer might be, 'So that I can leave a legacy and be remembered' or 'I would feel as though my life had had meaning'. Doing this will identify a more compelling purpose for you.

Kim Morgan and Geoff Watts,
authors of *The Coach's Casebook*

Worksheet – The confidence audit

Use the sheet to list the areas where you already have some confidence and areas where you would like to 'grow' your confidence.

Please include important hobbies, things that you love to do that aren't work related or that you 'used to be good at' when you were a child/younger – these may prove to be useful clues for some of the exercises later in the book...

I'M CONFIDENT HERE

NOTES

2 On quietness

> 'Quiet people have the loudest minds'
>
> Stephen Hawking

In an increasingly busy world, peace and quiet is a rare and precious commodity. Any quiet person knows that. I'm not sure that it is fully understood or accepted by others who are more gregarious. It's certainly not even on the horizon of loud tribal sorts who habitually talk loudly (often about themselves) and exhibit little awareness of the fact that if someone is sitting quietly it doesn't mean they have nothing going on in their heads. How many times have you had to move because someone has thoughtlessly polluted your thinking space?

Quietness can be misinterpreted in other ways. When I was at college there was a girl I knew who was friendly, quiet and well spoken, but who had little to say to me. I thought her aloof and that perhaps I was too worldly for her taste.

A couple of decades later, we bumped into each other. I mentioned my reflections only to find out that she felt exactly the same way. We were both shy. We both thought the other was aloof. In fact, we were both slightly terrified about talking to each other. Quietness has both benefits and pitfalls.

It's OK to be quiet.

Being a quiet soul is not always easy in practice. It's just not possible to avoid the sort of social and work oriented events that can prove so uncomfortable.

One can hardly wander round with a placard that says 'I'm a quiet, sensitive soul. Can we just hang out for a bit while I get my thoughts in line? Maybe let's sit and stare into space together for a while…'

This clearly doesn't make for a good networking experience.

What if… there's another way? What if there is a way to overcome the discomfort? Another way to get the ball rolling without a carefully rehearsed and hopelessly shallow elevator pitch?

What if it is as simple as employing your best listening skills and learning the art of well-crafted questions?

It's OK to be quiet, introverted, shy, retiring, unconfident, marching to a different drum. All of these things can be turned into advantages. The Art Of Shouting Quietly, in some senses, will encourage you to become ninja-like in the application of your strengths rather than fretting about your weaknesses.

It's OK to take your time.

Take as much as you need (within sensible limits).

Don't be pushed into reacting quickly to important challenges or questions – the world is already full of opinion pieces, snap judgment and sound bites.

Our world of pressure, deadlines, and competitive edge sadly lacks mindfulness, proper reflection and thoughtful, empathic dialogue. We get infected by ideas and carried along without time to reflect and make clear decisions about who we really are and what we really want in our lives.

You have the right to take your time.

Hidden strengths

Quiet people have hidden strengths. They are the dark horses who often come up trumps with a well-formed decision or a bit of razor sharp analysis just when it's needed most. They are better at weighing stuff up because there is less ego in the way. They don't muffle the evidence with shouting, posturing or improbable certainty about things. And quiet people persevere.

Examples of famous quiet people? Einstein, Susan Cain, Chopin, and Rosa Parks - all introverts. Ella Fitzgerald, Kiera Knightley, Tom Hanks - all self-confessed shy people. And a fair number more who have been diagnosed with social anxiety disorder and campaign on this issue.

All is not lost. It's perfectly possible to be shy, quiet, or introverted and get on in the world.

I often get to thinking that when the loudmouths have messed up the system it's the quiet, deep thinkers who will restore it.

The power of listening

One thing quiet people tend to be good at is listening. Dale Carnegie, in the seminal 'How To Win Friends And Influence People' espoused listening skills, coupled with great and genuine questions, as the means to get along in life.

We all love the sensation of being listened to. The more comprehensively we are listened to, the more we respond. It's powerful stuff. We fall in love with people who listen to us; we vote for people who listen to us, we buy the products and services of people who listen to us.

The ability to listen is one of the most profound influencing skills available to us.

Luckily, if you are a quiet soul, you are ahead of the game. The act of keeping one's mouth shut almost invariably makes you a better listener.

Mindfulness

Mindfulness is the art of paying attention. Mindfulness isn't just about listening - it's all about multi-sensory awareness and requires practice. In some senses, its closest relative is meditation. People who meditate are by nature mindful, but one can develop it as a skill in its own right. You can be mindful anywhere.

How can you promote yourself by paying attention to things? In the same way as we like people to listen, we love people to notice things. In my work as a coach, listening is useful but mindfulness is key. Noticing a sigh, a sharp intake of breath or a subtle movement or shift in posture can provide much more information than the verbal information that is freely offered.

The ability to practice mindfulness creates opportunity. Mindful people notice much more.

History speaks of sensitive people who seem more than usually alert to the nature of things.

Mindful people often notice things that our cluttered environment masks - it's as if they can cut through the white noise of day-to-day communication and filter out the important stuff.

Technology, stress, deadlines, and the all-pervading sense of urgency that is thrust upon us – these things mask signals and snippets of communication. Many aspects of our intuitive selves have been lost. Important signals lost in the fog. Mindfulness can help you recapture those things.

A short while ago, I was co-facilitating a leadership programme for a group of senior managers from a high street brand.

As part of the programme, we asked the group to work on their listening skills.

Cue eyes cast skyward. They had all done active listening/open questioning/you name it listening skills training before.

So... we asked them to listen to a colleague talking about a work issue for a minute or so using all their best listening skills. No doubt about it - they could all listen in the textbook active listening sense.

Then, we asked them to put their palms on their knees, close their eyes, breathe steadily and deeply for two minutes, and simply notice what was going on around them – the sounds, the smells, and the ambience of the room. We asked them to repeat the listening exercise. The noise levels in the room plummeted. The quality of listening was improved way beyond what they previously considered to be their high standard.

It only takes a couple of minutes to practice mindfulness - you can do it on the bus, on the train, whilst waiting for a meeting - and if all other attempts to find a quiet space defy you, in the loo. It prepares and readies you for situations that are difficult or that require your full attention.

Once you are able to easily put yourself into a mindful state, you can extend this technique into the realms of visualisation and mental rehearsal. Once in a mindful state it is much easier to mentally 'walk through' potentially stressful situations by first of all visualising them, then by rehearsing different scenarios within them – including how you are likely to feel and respond to the situation.

> **Action point:**
>
> Give yourself the gift of time to try this out.

Purpose, connectedness, sensitivity.

You don't need to be loud to display a solid sense of purpose. The words 'quiet' and 'determination' don't regularly crop up in the same sentence by accident.

Quiet people often display a sense of connectedness. It's as if they intuitively understand that in order to comprehend the whole, each of the constituent parts needs careful thought.

No accident then that the spiritual requirements of the world have been traditionally served by quiet contemplative souls.

Why does sensitivity get such bad press? I guess because it doesn't serve the needs of warmongering politicians or global capitalism very well. And it also serves as useful fulcrum for hateful behaviour towards anyone displaying any sort of liberal or non-conformist behaviours.

Let's face it - being sensitive, quiet or contemplative can set you aside from the mainstream. Unless, of course, you refuse to let that happen.

3 What moves you forward?

Chapter Three - What moves you forward? and Chapter Four, What holds you back? work in conjunction with each other. Knowing this stuff inside out will help you hit a breakthrough in your confidence levels and the way that you promote yourself.

The balance between these two opposing forces changes constantly – so it is vitally important to realise that the struggle to keep the two in balance is one that will be ongoing. It's not something that can be cured. Taking the time to understand yourself in this respect is time well spent. Taking time to get some feedback from others on this is also extremely useful. This may cause you some discomfort initially, but it's a price worth paying.

For example, Freud talked about the pain/pleasure principle - are you stirred into action by the anticipation of pleasure, or in order to avoid the pain that will be created by your inaction? For example, are you motivated more by the thought of accruing and saving money – or by doing what you need to do to avoid becoming overdrawn?

Understanding these motivational differences can make a huge difference to our wellbeing.

The building blocks of confidence

Here are the building blocks of confidence I referred to in the introduction. As you move through the book each of these points will be explored more fully:

Systematically reinforce your belief in yourself.

- By that I mean two things - getting to know who you really are and what you really want and need, and avoiding letting others interfere directly or indirectly with your actions and your innate sense of self.

Understand your place in the world - and what you were put on the planet to do.

- If you don't know who you are its hard to know what you should be doing in the world. How well developed is your innate sense of purpose? Are you a woman or man on a mission? In truth, many people simply never ask themselves this question.

- It requires intimate self-knowledge to get close to the answer. Those that do tackle this question often find themselves making radical changes.

Know what drives you forward and what holds you back – and how to keep these in balance.

- Get to know these opposing forces intimately and engage with them on a daily basis. Most of the people I know who are successful on their own terms understand that success comes through keeping these things in balance – and that it can be a struggle to do so.

Be true to yourself and your values.

- Your values are the energy behind your goals. It's hard to sustain any activity that isn't congruent with the personal values at your core. If you keep suffering from a sense of paralysis or keep grinding to a halt then the chances are that what you are doing is out of phase with your innate personal values. You may, unwittingly, be on the wrong path. This links to the next point...

Know that you have the power and freedom to shape your own sense of what is (and is not) possible.

- Be yourself in life – not what others think you should be. Avoid being influenced by other people's view of what is and isn't possible. I often work with people who have set off down one path because it was expected of them, or because it was what they were encouraged to do and actually it's not the path they would have chosen for themselves had they been left to follow their heart. There be dragons.

- If you are not flying, making progress, feeling at ease, ask yourself – are you where you are through choice, of your own free will, or because you have been directed there or are trying to please someone else?

Have a plan and a strong sense of purpose.

- Map out the things you want to achieve. Set goals, but don't fall into the trap of confusing the goal-setting with the action required to meet them – it's the action that counts, whether that is slow and steady or massive rapid change.

- If you find your goals intimidating, avoid 'rabbit in the headlights' syndrome - set smaller interim goals or simply move forward with the action one hop at a time. You'll get there in the end.

Know that asking for help is not an admission of failure – far from it!

- Asking for help is not an admission of failure – on the contrary it is a statement of courage, personal integrity, a willingness to change and move on. The funny thing is, when you display a readiness to be helped, help usually comes your way.

Develop the skill of asking for help in a structured way.

- Asking the right person the right question, in the right context, at the right time and in the right way will hugely increase your chances of getting the help you need. Later sections will explain how.

Know how to show up and share your gift in a way that sits comfortably with your values and mindset.

- What have you got that you can share with the world that has some real purpose and longevity to it – your legacy, if you like? What would you like to be remembered for?

It doesn't matter if you don't have a ready answer to all or even some of these questions right now. The point of this book is to help you think about these things and secure yourself some solid ground.

The clearer you become in terms of your self-knowledge and sense of purpose, the more confident you will become in promoting yourself. It will also become easier to rebuff your critics – who will always seize on a weak point or a display of indecision.

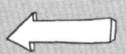

> **ACTION POINT:**
>
> Find someone to be accountable to who will help you stay on track. You can do the same for them. A fellow traveller. Avoid negative people who will collude with your inaction and aid and abet your procrastinations.

What does success mean to you?

It's really important not to fall into the trap of modelling yourself on someone else's idea of success. A hermit calligrapher living happily on a small amount, pursuing peace and self-sufficiency, is just as successful in my book as a businessperson with a multi-million pound turnover. If it's a get rich quick formula you are seeking you probably need to put this book down sharpish and find an online guru who'll be more than willing to let you join the queue and part with lots of money to learn 'the secret'!

The notion of success raises all sorts of interesting questions. Why? Because your chosen definition of success and your behaviour in business and in life should be defined by the values you espouse. In truth, it's your core values that should be driving everything along – more of that later.

Let me explain.

If you measure your success by the size of your income, then you'd better find something to do that meets a real demand. Something that people want, and what's more something that people will keep coming back for.

You need to stop wishing that one day you'll be discovered, or there will be a sudden surge in interest in your work, or that a wealthy patron will drop large and regular cheques through your letterbox. Yep, it happens now and again, but not to most common mortals.

It's what Alan Sugar calls 'smell and sell' – find the thing that you can supply that people really want. Green & Blacks use a similar process – literally get people to taste the product, and only then put time and money into developing the products that people like the taste of.

If you measure your success by celebrity, public profile, or notoriety, then you'd better not be a shrinking violet.

I meet people who don't seem to be terribly interested in getting rich, but who crave recognition. The thing that surprises me about this is how many folk who would really love to be recognised completely fail to push themselves forward. They do brilliant things or make fantastic and creative work, and share their ideas and talents with far too few people.

If you have a real contribution to make, the world will be pleased to hear about it, so don't hide your light under a bushel.

If success to you is having a peaceful life, simplify things. Live with a light touch, conserve energy, and respect others.

If success to you comes from the knowledge that you are making a contribution, helping change the world, creating pleasure, alleviating pain, creating a sense of wonder – any or all of these things – you are exactly the sort of person the world will reward in direct proportion to the contribution you make.

How we understand and internalize our measure of success helps set useful boundaries within which we can get focused, avoid distraction, and work towards goals that are based on the values we hold dearest.

For love or money

As well as having clear measures of what success means, it is key to understand the things that motivate you – do you respond to carrot or stick?

What satisfies you more – having people recognise and remark on your talents, financial rewards, regular positive feedback or the pure joy of the creativity in your work? Or do you negotiate (like most of us) a bit of a maze around a number of different pushes and pulls?

Do you find the rigour of working on 'bread and butter' tasks exciting, or does it dull your senses and blunt your imaginative edge?

The inbuilt problem for creative thinkers is that they are motivated more by intrinsic factors – the love of making things happen, the creative muse, the magic of it all coming together – and less by extrinsic factors like money and material rewards.

So how do you reconcile freedom of expression with the need to put food on the table?

I'm not going to try and provide an answer here – every single person I work with resolves this in different ways. But the realisation that some degree of separation between the work that you do for money, and the work that you do for love, might actually be quite healthy, can be freeing in an odd sort of way!

The clincher for me is this - the people that consistently do the work they love in an uncompromised way, and work with authenticity and passion as a result, usually end up harvesting richer rewards than those who doggedly try to link the monetary reward directly to the creativity.

This can be resolved. A little support, analysis and honest feedback can go a long way!

Dealing with 'The Proper Job' putdown

Self-employment gets bad press. If you tell someone that you're going it alone the chances are you'll hear choruses of:

'Why don't you get a proper job?'..... 'Isn't that really just a hobby?'..... 'How will you ever earn a decent living doing that?'

Heartbreaking, isn't it? Especially when the questions come from your own friends or family. Or worse still – from your partner.

And yet it's one of the most prominent themes I deal with within my mentoring sessions – solopreneurs whose confidence has been battered by folk who simply don't seem to understand that a self-determined life is a valid career choice.

It is a valid choice. You have every right to choose to earn your living – at whatever scale you want to operate – in the way you want to.

It may not be what your parents envisioned. It may not earn you a fortune. But it's a valid, worthwhile, life-affirming choice.

So how do you convince the skeptics around you? Convince them that you are doing the right thing with your life? In truth, you shouldn't have to. Really.

It's not a job. It's a vocation. It's a calling. Most of the truly creative people I know would continue to be creative even if there was no money left in the world.

Creativity was born out of necessity – it's an instinct. Without creativity we could not survive. We wouldn't have the skills and tools we need to keep ourselves alive.

I once shocked a local authority arts officer by saying that creative people were like cockroaches* - what I meant was this: Even if a bomb were to drop, if a holocaust tore through the civilised world, if all systems were disrupted, all communications severed, creative people would emerge and rebuild with whatever they could find. And they would rebuild something awesome.

(*Cockroaches are renowned for their ability to survive extreme events)

People need to be reminded that everything they pick up and use, sit on, watch, listen to, read, purchase, travel in or on, live in, cook and eat with has had the touch of an artist, writer or designer, engineer or architect along the way. And many of those creative souls live non-conventional lives.

Many have starved or failed at points in their career. But we have what we have because someone else did what they had to do – often in the face of extreme doubt and criticism.

So – you don't have to take the criticism. You don't have to justify what you do. You don't have to listen to the disappointment of others. Empathise with their fears and concerns – because that's often what drives the nagging from parents, siblings and spouses. Understand where they are coming from by all means. They may be justifiably worrying how the rent will be paid. They may be fearful of their own creativity, or be grieving the lack of it. Sometimes it's best not to know.

Be proud. Be yourself. You are entitled to that. Live the creative life. Take risks.

We'd be living much poorer lives in a much poorer society if it weren't for people like you.

Your story

You owe it to yourself to send out the most compelling message about yourself, your product and services that you can.

Not everyone is a natural writer or teller of stories. However, there are a few things you simply have to do if you are going to inspire and enthuse people to buy, recommend, or review and promote your products and services.

You need to:
- Find your voice – tell your story as opposed to talking about yourself.
- Tell the stories of the things you do and why – what inspires and influences you and the beliefs and values that drive you.

- Give your customers and/or collaborators something they can connect to and feel empathy with.
- Build relationships rather than making individual sales.
- Decide on the right medium to use to tell your stories – face to face, the web, social media, video, or the printed page.

Stories are the currency of human relationships. The most valuable bits of our history, culture and value systems get transmitted through storytelling. Why produce a generic brochure, website or postcard, when the thing that will sell your work, over and over again, and will enthuse people to talk about it to each other thereby transmitting it virally, and will add value (I mean real cash value) to your work – is the story behind it and the person who conceived it.

People need to 'get' your values straight away. How can you represent your values in words and images, smells, textures and sound?

You need to be clear about this because different people will receive and decode your message in different ways. Some people are predominantly visual thinkers, some predominantly auditory - focusing first on text and spoken word. Others are kinesthetic, liking video, involvement, and things to do and interact with. It's no accident that video is the most popular medium on the web. It can be used to satisfy all of these learning styles.

I'd rather sit and talk to an entrepreneur about how to develop the story of their work than talk about marketing theory. The theory is useless without the substance. I'm spending much more of my time now working on this, because it is really important – for individuals and organisations alike.

Remember – you are not necessarily aiming for a slick elevator pitch, just a genuine 'to the point' short story that will engage and create empathy.

Your creative DNA

When you boil everything down to the essentials, what's at the core of your creative being?

I'm going to pose a few questions here. You can address them one at a time, in any order you wish. The questions are prompts to get you to thinking about some really important stuff, like:

What is it about you that connects you to people? What is it about you and your work that people can empathise with? What do you do that resonates with their values?

Ninja Tip - Seizing opportunities

One morning, whilst listening to the local news the presenter mentioned that later in the week they would be talking about the sensitive subject of Planning a Funeral. As I make ceramic funerary urns and memory boxes I thought that this might be something that I could be involved with. I sent an email and to my surprise and delight got a reply asking me to telephone the radio station and arrange for a reporter to come and see my work and interview me.

A new experience can be scary, but because I knew what I could achieve using clay and importantly, how and why I make the work, I was prepared. And that's what I'd like to pass on to you - be prepared and when the opportunities come along you can grasp them confidently.

Ann Bates
ceramicist

Worksheet - You and your values

Try and identify your personal core values. What are the main drivers in the work that you do? What do you have strong feelings, opinions or beliefs about?

For example, are you passionate about saving the planet? Do you want to use your skills to improve people's environment? Is the love of nature a powerful driver for you, or the love of particular materials or aesthetic considerations?

Use the worksheet to identify and list all the things that are most important to you — the things that get you out of bed in the morning.

Can you identify a top 3?

NOTES

OP 3 VALUES ?

TRADITION

COMMUNITY

QUALITY

WHAT ARE YOUR T

AESTHET

ENVIRONMENT

DESIGN

SAV
THE
PLAN

NOTES

Point to ponder:

In some businesses, the person is the brand. Is this the case for you? What if your brand values need to be different? How would you describe them?

Point to ponder:

If you/your brand were a stick of seaside rock, what would be written through the core of you? Can you think of between one and four words that sum this up? Play around with this idea over a period of a day or two. Draw a series of circles on a large sheet of paper and sketch out your responses as if you were looking at the rock in cross section. The things you write can be practical, enigmatic, symbolic, and descriptive - try approaching this from a number of different angles.

What do people love about what you do? What do they love enough to want more of?

4 What holds you back?

It is only by truly understanding and embracing the things that hold you back that you will make sustained progress. Otherwise it's a bit like a doctor treating symptoms not causes. This section of the book looks at a range of things that get in the way. I have two reasons for bringing these things into play. First, because you need to name the beasts that hold you back. Second, you need to figure out how to avoid them, live with them, or put them to death.

For example, I used to be a serial procrastinator. At first, I was unaware of that fact. When I did become aware, I did little about it. Other people became dissatisfied with my procrastinating. I had to deal with it. I made lists and habitually moved things from one list to another; I created charts and conveniently filed them away. I put notes on my computer and forgot what I called them.

Procrastination is a bit like the mythical Hydra – remove one ugly head and several grow back in its place.

You need to fight total war on a number of fronts and change tactics daily in order to stay ahead of the game. Procrastination is bad enough if you are in control of you own destiny - if other blocks are in play, then it changes the game somewhat.

Value/goal conflicts

It is important to understand that your values generate the energy that fuels you to work consistently towards meeting your goals. Do something that fits with your innate values and you will make progress. Do something that doesn't fit and you will grind to a halt. It's a no brainer.

One way to judge whether an activity fits with your innate values is the extent to which you are in flow whilst you are doing it – does time pass without you noticing it? Are you eager to get back to the task after taking a break? Do you consistently look forward to your next burst of activity?

If the answer to these questions is yes, then the chances are your chosen activity meshes with your core values. If the answer is no, then goals and values are in conflict.

It's important to work from a baseline of strong personal values – and values that are your own – neither pushed upon you by others nor acquired by osmosis through the ever-present 'collective unconscious' of social media overwhelm.

We get infected by ideas and carried along without time to reflect and make clear decisions about who we really are and what we really want in our lives.

Why does this matter?

Without clear insight as to what's really at the core of you – the real you – life becomes a struggle. Your goals and values are in conflict with each other. If you are conflicted, it's hard to project a version of yourself to others that they can trust and empathise with.

Without empathy, you won't get the quality of relationship you need to build the partnership, move the project along or make the sale.

Point to ponder:

Are your goals and values complementary?

Unrealised potential

Metaphorically speaking we all come into life with the seed of something significant within us. This seed of honest potential, if it gets enough light, nutrients and nurture allows us to grow tall, put down roots and become what we really ought to be.

If the seed doesn't get the right balance of light, nutrients and nurture it fails to thrive. We don't grow straight, true and vigorous in the way we ought to have done. We don't put down the substantial roots.

It doesn't take much – strong parental views perhaps, both positive and negative; over-protection or neglect; critical comments from significant adults or our siblings; having our natural talents dismissed in favour of other people's career preferences maybe - to conspire to stunt this growth. We may have illnesses or critical events in play that throw us off course. I had two significant childhood illnesses – one that nearly killed me (or so I was told) and one that was recurring and painful over a number of years. All sorts of things can pull the rug out from under our feet.

We can be led away from our innate talents and abilities in one fell swoop (a parent telling us we are useless) or over a long period of time (when a chronic illness or pain saps the will to live). Sometimes it's a combination of events and influences that conspire to set us off on the wrong foot.

In truth an awful lot of the worst criticism and misinformation often comes from people who would regard themselves as truly well meaning and with our best interests at heart. So we trust, we conform, or we fall into the path of least resistance. Or all of the above.

The trouble is, the faulty beliefs that are generated this way are what we become used to and our easy familiarity with them is hard to give up. This, after all, is the self we have become in order to survive.

In my work as a coach I often work with people who are struggling with the growing tension created by the knowledge that their real potential has not been fully realised, and a growing realisation that the script they have been following was never really of their own making. They have been surviving with a version of themselves that is a far cry from their innate potential - had it been allowed to evolve freely.

No wonder then that as we mature and our self-knowledge increases, we may feel a tugging towards something new and indefinable – a yearning for change. A strong frustration that things are not right – or indeed have never felt right. This existential disarray bubbling under the surface plays havoc with our sense of purpose, sense of direction and inner confidence to boot.

The sense of disarray feeds behaviour:

- Not standing up for yourself because you've been conditioned to rank other people's priorities and opinions above your own.

- Becoming perfectionist – always on the lookout for the right answer, the right arrangement, and the right response from others. Other's standards and behaviour constantly fall short of your expectations.

- Rejecting compliments, or worse still, reading them as direct criticism.

- Constantly putting things off. Nothing seems to fit or feel right, so nothing gets done.

- Inability to allow yourself to take credit for your talents and achievements, instead thinking you will be found out, or that you are somehow fraudulent.

- Struggling to get out into the stretch zone as a result of being told that things are beyond your capacity. I knew someone who was told he should get a career standing outside a post office with his tongue out – so people could dampen their postage stamps on it prior to posting their letters. He left home, went to sea at 16, and rose through the ranks to command a ship.

You develop a mental filter conditioned by past experience, that conditions the brain to look out for familiar signs and act accordingly. If you are used to conflict you will find conflict. If you are used to criticism, you will find criticism in what others say to you.

What does not change is the seed of honest potential. It's still there.

That's the quest – find what's at the core of you, tease it out, give it the nutrients it needs. Regenerate.

But first, lets take a closer look at a few more of the blocks.

Impostor syndrome

According to Wikipedia, impostor syndrome, or fraud syndrome, is a psychological phenomenon in which people are unable to internalize their accomplishments. Despite external evidence of their competence, those with the syndrome remain convinced that they are frauds and do not deserve the success they have achieved.

Proof of success is dismissed as luck, timing, or as a result of deceiving others into thinking they are more intelligent and competent than they believe themselves to be. As such it can stop us in our tracks – we are not worthy, so we don't push ourselves forward on more prominent platforms. We fail to 'stick our head above the parapet'.

Hmmm... familiar?

Although it's not a recognised psychological disorder, it manifests itself powerfully in the lives of a lot of creative people.

Sometimes it's a minor hurdle – and simply reminding ourselves that it's largely just another threshold of anxiety to be stepped over on a daily basis does the trick. For others it's a fairly constant companion, and a measurable hindrance to progress.

So how can we overcome this barrier to self-development? The first step is to recognise that it is happening and to accept that we have to factor it in rather than ignore or deny it.

The second step is to figure out just how it gets in the way – what's it stopping us doing?

The third step is to strategise – how do we behave, how do we plan, what support and advice do we seek in order to tiptoe round it or break through it?

Metaphorically speaking, we need to identify and name the beast before we can kill it.

This is not an easy task. When I'm out on the road delivering talks and workshops to creative people I often note that it's usually not the quality of work that holds people back – rather the quality of their courage and ambition. My advice? Be bold – aim high.

Surround yourself with supportive people; find someone close to be accountable to. Ask them to help you whilst you undertake the challenge, and keep nudging you now and again to keep on track. This accountability alone can often make the difference between success and failure.

> **Action point:**
>
> Make a list of all the people who are most supportive of your hopes and dreams.

Toxic relationships and blame

Toxic relationships create misery. Relationships can go bad, or they can get off on the wrong foot in the first place (easily done).

Toxic relationships and quiet people don't mix. And quiet, tolerant, sensitive souls have a tendency to accept otherwise unacceptable environments - be that at work or at home. The reasons for that are endless and it's not the job of this book to explore that.

The ability to see both sides of any given situation can be a double-edged sword. If you are a sensitive empathic soul, you may tend to give other people the benefit of the doubt to the extent that you cancel out your own needs and requirements. The danger then is that you become thwarted and resentful rather than assertively sticking up for your own preferences. This can turn into an internalised battle.

This will exhaust you. It's all too much to carry in your head. It can become obsessive, with thoughts circling around unresolved.

Don't blame others for your own lack of progress. Your progress is your own responsibility.

There are three main options open when toxicity and blame are at play:

1. Accept things as they are.
2. Change things for the better.
3. Move on, take time to find what you really want, and develop the life you really deserve.

Nothing is permanent. Moving on can be liberating.

Beware the well-intentioned critic

I've been writing and talking a lot recently about the things that motivate us as creative beings - and the things that hold us back. I never expected for a moment that I would discover that, many years ago, I had unwittingly fallen foul of one of the very things I had been warning others to avoid.

Picture this: A warm sunny day at 'Ceramics in Charnwood'. It's a lovely annual event in the spacious town centre market place, featuring potters and ceramic artists from all over the country. It's both popular and well attended.

My partner spotted a polite crocodile-shaped queue of children waiting to have a go on Loughborough potter

Bridget McVey's portable electric wheel. We stopped to watch a few wobbly pots being thrown and Janet said to me 'You used to do that, didn't you?' (It's over 30 years since I threw a pot), followed by a gentle shove in the direction of the queue.

I was once quite proficient on the wheel having learned to throw at school, followed by a summer internship at Govancroft Pottery in Glasgow - long since demolished, but famous for hand thrown whisky flagons and in the 70's for a rather funky range of domestic stoneware. I'll pick up on that part of the story in a moment.

Despite my fluttered protestations, Janet and Bridget by now had me seated at the wheel resplendent in flowery apron and with a ball of clay. What happened next was both simple and profound. I remembered how to throw and managed to produce a quite respectable small pot. By far the more important revelation was the fact that whilst throwing I dropped into a deeply satisfying zone I had long since forgotten. Why had I simply stopped doing this all those years ago?

I went to Art College in the 70's with the intention of studying ceramics. Whilst working at Foundation level I had regular pottery sessions, which I loved and saw as the preparation for a Degree level ceramics course.

However, in the 70's wheel thrown ware had fallen from grace. Slip casting, slabbing and sculptural ware had become more fashionable. One of my tutors - someone who I had a great deal of respect for - said to me one day 'Peter, throwers are two a penny these days. If you want to succeed in ceramics you must explore other ways of producing work'. I was 18, and impressionable. It was one of those killer comments that stuck. I was put off throwing, became disillusioned, focused on painting and drawing instead and chose a degree in Fine Art.

I didn't really question what happened at the time, but sitting at the wheel in the marketplace brought a whole raft of questions into play - what if I'd brushed off the comment and carried on making pots? Where would I be now?

So now to the real point of my story. All too often a well-meaning person of importance - parent, spouse, sibling, teacher - questions our natural choice. We get knocked off course. We adopt someone else's notion of what we might be or become and end up not doing the things we were put on the planet to do.

This troubles a fair number of the creative people that I coach. If they have managed to set off down the right route they are often hounded by well intentioned critics (why don't you get a proper job, isn't that just a hobby, why don't you train as/marry a lawyer etc.) and if not they feel at odds with the role they currently occupy because it's not their true calling. From a coaches point of view it's a difficult one to set straight.

It's no accident that people often re-confront their thwarted creativity later in life - as a mid life career change or a plausible retirement decision.

This can create turbulence not just for the individual but for those around them too.

It's vital to be yourself, not what others think you should be. It's also important not to allow others to infect you with their 'impossibility' mindset. It may sound cynical but I think that many critics speak from a baseline of their own thwarted ambitions.

Does any of this resonate with you in some way? Has your progress been impeded by others? Or do you recognise the protective 'parent' behaviour in yourself?

The first bit of progress I think comes in simply recognising that these issues affect you in some way. The next comes in figuring out what, if anything, you need to do about it. Some simply recognise, shrug their shoulders and move on. Some seek out positive thinkers - radiators, I call them - to benefit from the mutual encouragement, support and accountability that comes from sharing plans and ambitions with others who are in a similar process of change.

Some get stuck, and the stuckness is a source of real discomfort. Symptoms include a sense of not being true to oneself, of being out of step, of wading through treacle. Real energy and motivation comes when personal goals, values and what you are doing with your life are all aligned.

This deeply personal creativity needs to be celebrated, practised and unleashed. It doesn't matter if you are 7 or 70 - if it's in you, let it out. Whatever happens, don't let it be someone else's thoughtless but well-intentioned words that stop you or put a brake on you practising your craft (however that manifests itself for you) to the best of your abilities.

The internal management committee

Imagine this: Everyone has an internal management committee. Most of us unconsciously run our decisions past a number of influential characters in our lives. We think about what they might think about our decisions, and modify our actions accordingly. Who is on the committee? The makeup of the committee is different for everyone. For some, our fathers or mothers may dominate, for others our partners, siblings, bosses, opinionated aunties or uncles, or the dog (I'm serious).

This phenomenon runs to extremes.

People will refuse to remove themselves from danger in order to protect the people or things they love or for which they feel a sense of responsibility. In the major flooding that affected parts of the UK 2014, when confronted with a stark choice, people would stay in a flooded house rather than abandon a pet.

Captains go down with ships - they are expected to, are they not?

The internal management committee can create huge conflicts. When opinions and loyalties differ, who do we listen to? This can tear people apart, often resulting in paralysis. Who do you please?

The obvious answer is that you must please yourself first. You are, after all, the Chief Executive of your own life!

What others think and say.

> 'O would some power the giftie gie us
> to see ourselves as others see us'
>
> To a Louse – Robert Burns

To what extent does it matter what others think? How much attention should we pay to that? At one extreme, if a toxic relationship leads to you losing friends and creating chilly wastes between yourself and your family, then it's clearly time to sit up, listen to what's going on and wrestle back control of your life.

At the other end of the scale, in day to day terms, the danger is that we simply choose to let things drift, fail in the quality of our mindfulness and attention, and fail to catch the smaller signs and regular feedback from others that should help us adjust our behaviour and stay on course.

It's part laziness, partly environment, and partly our reptilian brain holding us back from making change. Change rocks the boat. Change sometimes spells danger. It just seems much easier not to go there.

On a personal level, we pretty much all know individuals who are destined for an unhappy and bitter old age because they can't or won't behave consistently in a socially acceptable way – like being able to adapt to circumstances, apologise or take other's feelings and opinions into account.

On a business level, a similar inability to adapt can spell the end – only it's both the product and the business owner's behaviour that need to evolve sometimes – hanging on to tired old products and ideas, or failing to spot changing trends and, crucially, to act/change/adapt early enough.

The trick is to adopt change, not stasis, as the normal state of things. Making lots of little changes works just as well as making great big radical changes. Both approaches have their benefits.

We've had masses of change thrust upon us throughout this last recession – and we know there's more to come. We can stubbornly resist, or adapt and learn new ways of thinking and acting, or we can become the change itself, each of us contributing what we can to bring about positive change – in ourselves, through our businesses and on into the world at large.

The first step is simply paying attention. What others think is part – but only part – of that.

Point to ponder:

We can't control what others say or do – but we can control our own response to it. How we choose to respond can change the outcomes for better or worse.

Ninja Tip - Talking in public

I honestly think the phrase 'no one cares' helps a lot. Take the pressure off yourself by seeing your problems from a stranger's viewpoint.

When I'm onstage, the worst thing that happens is I bore someone for 20 mins. They can live with that. Being an idiot is ok, in fact...it is more charming and endearing than being a perceived 'winner'.

So, enjoy losing. Or rather, enjoy the process and don't invest your emotions too strongly on the outcome.

Iszi Lawrence,
stand up comedian, historian, podcaster

Worksheet – Deciding priorities

Maintaining focus is a huge struggle. And even when you think you've got it nailed, lack of focus returns – sneaking back up on you stealthily. And it's exactly at the point when you're struggling to focus that your self-discipline and best intentions tend to desert you. Whatever you use to get clarity again, it has to be simple, straightforward and downright easy to use.

Here's a technique I use when I can't see the wood from the trees. It's one of those things that is simultaneously stupidly simple and totally profound. I hope you enjoy it.

On the 'Towards' side, write down the things that you want more of in your life – or that you want to move towards. Better ways of doing things, new ways of working, things you want to spend more time on, or that redress the balance in your life in a positive way.

On the 'Away From' side, write down things that you want to get rid of or move away from – things that sap your energy, that no longer float your boat, bits of redundant attitude, or things (or maybe people) that distract you.

Work quickly and intuitively – listen to the inner voice that sometimes is a bit reluctant to speak up. The 'More of' / 'Move Towards' side will tell you what you need to focus on.

NOTES

AWAY FROM

TOWARDS

NOTES

5 Possibility

> Don't let others project their impossibilities onto your life. You have the power and the right to create your own framework of possibility.

Early on in my career, I worked in New York for a while. The experience totally changed my view of what it is possible to do with a life. I found myself exposed, for the first time in my life, to an overwhelming 'can do' mindset.

All over the place, people saying YES! to ideas. It was warm, wonderful and transforming. This was not British. This was something very different, very open and very affirming. I went hoping for a bit of experience and advice and came home with a business transformed and enough ideas and energy to keep me fuelled for the next couple of years. People didn't just help me - they stayed up late teaching me things, and gave me ideas. They also taught me how to collaborate with others for mutual gain, and above all how to ask for help without feeling like some weakling social pariah.

I carry these ideas with me and I try wherever possible to encourage people to think in this way. More things are possible than you can ever imagine. Helping others strengthens your own position and carries you onwards. Asking for help is a good move - always (more on that later). Give ideas the oxygen they need until they fly. If they don't work don't squander precious resources keeping them on life support. And don't grieve for ideas that don't work - internalise the learning and get on with newer better ones.

The Art of the Possible

As a specialist coach, I approach clients in the hope that I can work with them to establish a framework of possibility. This is basically about helping them see their goals not as vague options for some future version of their life, but as achievable and possible, with some steps that can be taken right here and right now to move towards them.

Don't deny your shortcomings - work with them. This mindset of possibility sets you up with a much greater chance of success - especially if you've done some work around identifying and removing blocks, and on putting the right support mechanisms in place.

Embrace your non-conformity

Instead of looking at super-confident people and wasting time wishing you could be like them, embrace your non-conformity, be true to yourself and do what you want. I don't mean embark on a trail of literal or metaphorical destruction. I mean do what you want for the benefit of yourself and others.

My Dad, bless him, had a mantra: 'Don't wish your life away son, do something!' Of course, it's only in the light of adulthood that I finally got what he meant.

He knew I didn't get it, of course, and instead embarked on a mission of helping me experience things and try stuff out. He always focused on giving me experiences and meeting people - not buying me things. He knew I was marching to a different drum even then and wanted me to be prepared.

Free yourself from 9-5 thinking

Allow yourself the freedom to work at the times that enable flow and allow you to be most productive. I know successful people that work from home but who wear smart clothes every day and get to their home office desk at 8.30 every morning. Others I know don't get up until 10am and are at their most productive during the second half of the day.

Think about it. People already work across all sorts of time zones and shift patterns anyway. Map out your personal Hot-Spots - the time slots where you work most efficiently during the day. You may also find different tasks easier at different times of the day.

I find that dealing with incoming and outgoing mail first thing works best for me – then other more creative tasks are not conducted with the thought of admin weighing on my mind. I write most productively mid to late afternoon and then again later in the evening.

Observing what you do best at particular times of day and then allocating your workload accordingly can really boost your confidence. You will feel that things flow better, that you achieve more and that you are not pushing against a dead weight of resistance because you are trying to do the wrong thing at the wrong time.

Evaluate your strengths

A few pages back we explored the Impostor Syndrome. In order to combat this tendency to diminish our achievements and strengths it is really important to identify, acknowledge and internalise the strengths that you already have.

The first step is to create an inventory of your strengths, skills, knowledge and experience.

Worksheet - The Reverse Timeline

The reverse timeline is a great way to think about what has worked best for you in the past. Begin by photocopying the worksheet - or draw your own version.

Part One:

This is an exercise in remembering. Starting from today, work backwards. Try to remember all the significant events that have been really positive milestones in your life/career development.

What are all the things that you have done or achieved that have contributed to you getting to where you are now?

Each time something significant occurs to you, note it down. Go back as far as you can – maybe even to things that you did in childhood. What are the 'stand out' moments?

Then work back to today, deciding which of these 'best bits' you need to capture so you can remember the value of them and bring those strengths back into play wherever you can.

Part Two: Your 'Best Bits'

Gather together all the feedback that people have given you - testimonials, press cuttings, assessments, evaluations, Twitter or Facebook comments even. Create a physical file, collect or create digital images or scan paper documents. In effect, what you want to create is a virtual treasure chest of all the things you have done and all the good comments people have made about what you do.

There are two powerful reasons for doing this. The first is that it gives you the ability to reflect on the great things you have done and that you are capable of. The second is that should you need source material for marketing purposes, you have it ready and waiting.

It's really important that you have this evidence - because when you are feeling low, crestfallen or disappointed it will bolster you up and give you the confidence to dust yourself down and enter the fray once more.

6 What are you on the planet to do?

A lot of people go through life without ever answering this question. I use the phrase 'true north' - others might use the words mission or quest or direction or spiritual journey.

Where, in the end, do you want your life's journey to take you? It's a big, fat, overwhelming question. At the beginning of his life, my father's quest was to travel the world. He did so. At the end of his days his quest was for personal peace and quiet - and for his family to find love, happiness and security. Our definition of true north changes as we grow and change. What is it for you, right here, right now?

This is an important question. You should feel moved to action by your answer.

Having a clear idea of where your 'true north' lies is one of the major underpinnings of confidence in yourself and your actions. It's the point from which you calibrate your compass for everything else in life.

Cardinal Points

If we can stay with the compass metaphor a little longer, the next question I'd like to pose is this: What are the cardinal points on your compass? What are the moral and ethical points of reference? Again, being sure of these instills confidence. One of the attributes that all great leaders have shared is moral certainty.

What are your boundaries? What will and won't you do? Knowing what you will happily say yes to, and what you will refuse, and why, helps you set an accurate course.

What's Your Gift?

> 'What you do for yourself dies with you –
> what you do for others lives on and is immortal'
>
> Alfred Paine

Once you have established a clear view of who you are and where you are heading, then the next question is this: What's your gift?

Once all the clutter is cleared away and you are thinking about this from your own clear and unhindered point of view, what do you really want to contribute to the world? How would you like to be remembered?

Do you want to write, compose, or heal? Do you want to paint 'plein air' around the world? Do you want to interview the last remaining crew from the WW2 bomber command

and make a film about them? Do you want to run spiritual retreats on a wild and remote Greek island? Do you want to be the world's premier expert on ray guns? Save swimmer's lives with a solar powered surfboard? Change lives with an invention? These are real examples - all people I know and have met or worked with.

The world is your oyster, and your quietness, shyness, introversion or current lack of confidence should not be a barrier to you.

What's your gift to the world? Once you have defined it, the rest of this book will help you find the means to package and deliver it.

How big is your world?

To be truly confident, you need to engage with this question on both very practical and deeply metaphorical levels.

In my life I have rubbed shoulders with people who have never been to the seaside. I have also rubbed shoulders with people who have crossed every ocean. It's not my business to compare one with the other in a critical way but I must ask the question: 'Are your boundaries there through choice or habit or circumstance or... what?'

For many years, I worked as an artist in schools in the UK. My mental map of the world was limited by my drive time. Occasionally I'd work outside my region, and I always jumped at the chance, but it usually involved what I considered to be long journeys. My mental map had limiting beliefs attached to it.

Time spent working in America resulted in my mental map of the world being changed forever. New York to Washington – 4 hours – was regarded as a short drive and clients, without a second thought, absorbed the cost of travel and overnight stays. I swore when I came home after the first trip that geography would not be a limiting factor in the success of my business.

The costs and logistics of travel and overseas delivery have altered radically. It annoys me that I can book a week's holiday in Greece, including flights, for the same price as a peak time rail return between my hometown and London. Rather than being frustrated and flummoxed by these crazy paradoxical things, we should embrace them.

You may have good reasons for not wanting to sail the seven seas, but we now have other ways of connecting locally, regionally, and globally. You can change what you choose to do. You can form different, more ambitious habits; you can work within even the most challenging circumstances to make extraordinary things happen.

A few years ago, I started a Facebook group (The Art of Work – Fresh Thinking for Creative People). It now has an active membership of artists, makers and other creatives from all over the world. People have met, shared information and collaborated simply by meeting others in the group.

I use Twitter to connect with other creative people across the globe, and as a result have sent books to readers in almost every continent. I now write for The Cape Craft and Design Institute in Cape Town, in South Africa. A tweet led to a book sale, the book sale led to a writing gig. My next thought: How can I turn the writing gig into an opportunity to visit Cape Town?

The world is indeed your oyster.

What's your geography?

I once mentored a really talented textile artist who was struggling to earn a living. Her work was great; she had a lovely studio and workshop from which she ran courses for small groups.

When I asked her where she advertised, it turned out that she was targeting locally. She simply was not spreading her net far enough. We took out a map and did a calculation based on an hour's drive time and found that there were a number of large population centres within that range from which she could attract a much bigger customer base.

Whatever you do - be you an IT specialist, copywriter, musician or designer - you need to figure out how far you need to spread your wings in order to get the profile and/or income you need. Are you comfortable holding a globe in your hands and saying 'all of it' or is your map a continent, country or regional map?

If someone rang you tomorrow and said "if you can get to Tokyo for 10 days, we can give you work and teach you all you need to know" would you be open, ready and willing to grab that opportunity?

Cool things like that do happen (I'll tell you how you can make this more likely) and you need to be ready.

Worksheet – How BIG is your World?

Use the worksheet to make notes, or draw your own diagram on a large sheet of paper.

Where in the world do you want your voice to be heard? Where do you want to practice your craft? Where do you want your products and services to be seen? (This question should address both where you want your presence to be felt and where your clients, actual and potential, may be.)

Local, Regional, National, Global, Interplanetary?

NOTES

HOW BIG IS YOUR WORLD?

NOTES

7 Embracing Risk - The Risk/Reward ratio

Foolishly, some people think that eradicating risk entirely is the best way to proceed with the greatest confidence. But what kind of opportunities then remain for you to be confident with? Much diminished ones, I fear. The best way to proceed with confidence is to properly assess risk, and to do this thoroughly. Don't for goodness sake, put your head in the sand and ignore risk entirely.

We all have to take risks sometimes. I've witnessed people taking all kinds of risks – some calculated, some foolish. I'm not sure how many of them actually thought through their actions in advance.

I don't think that everyone really evaluates the risks they take on a day-to-day basis – the danger in thinking too hard about all of this is that you simply end up not doing anything at all.

Risk isn't just about money either – we can lose valuable time, risk our reputation, and take risks with our physical and mental well-being. Being self-employed means you have to be prepared to embrace all of these things.

My aim in writing this is to encourage you to think in simple terms about the risk/reward ratio – in other words, what you are likely to get back from the time, money and emotion you put into any specific bit of development.

I'd like to give a few examples of the types of risk I see, and then move on to thinking about how to mitigate those risks in order to make life a little more comfortable.

Spending too much too soon

I often see people investing far too much in ideas before they are properly tested – in particular taking on office space or making large capital investments before the business idea has been properly tested and proven.

A similar thing happens with marketing. People assume that they can't get started without an expensive suite of marketing materials, and spend hundreds of pounds, if not more, on glossy promo materials. And then there's the expensive websites…

Cutting corners

There's a powerful temptation to do everything yourself – especially if you can't afford to invest much at the beginning. You print your own marketing materials, construct your own website and do your own accounting. This raises two really important issues – first, are you capable of doing these things well; and second, are they in truth false economies?

Too many non-designers try to do their own graphic design. Too many non-techies try to create their own websites, and - how many of us really know from year to year just what and how much we can claim as legitimate expenses against tax? If we do invest time in becoming expert in all these areas, what happens to the time we should be spending on our creative practice?

The 'I need to do my books, get these flyers out, get my website updated' statements become at best indicators of too much time displaced into non-creative activities and at worst a clear symptom of rampant procrastination.

Failing to take professional advice

Taking professional advice at the appropriate time can make the difference between success and failure. It can stop you falling foul of the law, and it can reduce the risk of your work being copied or hi-jacked in other ways.

Good specialist business advice – from an accountant, or around copyright and design rights, or in relation to branding and visual identity – can often repay your investment many times over in addition to reducing the risks I have outlined above. It's simply foolish to try to be your own expert in all matters.

Risk to reputation

Think carefully about getting into situations that might tarnish your reputation. When I'm asked to collaborate, I always check out the potential partners first. Do they deliver to a high quality and will they command the respect of my audience too? What if one of the partners fails to deliver – would that affect me by association? Reputation is all – people are quick to move on if they get a hint that you have a weak spot anywhere.

So how do you cut the risks and reap the rewards?

First, you need to get your head around the risk/reward ratio in relation to each new thing you do. Will the effort, cash or emotional investment be repaid in such a way as to make it all worthwhile?

Second, you need to think clearly before making an investment – what is the minimum viable investment you can make in order to test the market – not just for your overall business idea, but for each product or service before you roll it out?

The notion of minimum viable effort and investment is important. This is not about cutting corners – it is about understanding exactly how much or little it is sensible to risk at each stage of development. Do you need a ten page website or could you test your idea on a blog or Facebook page first? Do you need to borrow lots of money, or could you fund a test out of cash flow initially, and then put in the money when you are more certain of a good outcome? I'm sure you can see what I mean.

Test things thoroughly

Big companies test ideas relentlessly. Why should we behave differently?

It's easy to do this nowadays and social media provides the perfect platform to pose questions, post images and ask opinions. The perfect outcome of market research is to sell products or get serious enquiries while you are still in the market research phase.

Test new ideas by creating a 'minimum viable product'. This is a version of your product idea that does not require a massive investment of money or time. Try this minimum version out on real people and get as much feedback as you can. This will tell you if your investment is going to pay off – or not, as the case may be.

Dare to be different.

Dare to present your ideas differently. In terms of self-promotion this differentiation is key to your success.

Risk is unavoidable

It doesn't matter how risk averse you are. Risk is unavoidable. Just don't lock yourself away through fear of making a mistake. Every mistake we make gets us closer to where we need to be.

Risk reaps rewards

Nothing ventured, nothing gained. We know that those who take risks tend to reap the highest rewards. The trick is not to gamble with anything that you can't afford to lose. The cleverest people are the ones who get huge rewards from low risk enterprises. They test wisely and modestly until they are sure the idea will work, and then they roll it out, stage by stage, testing and proving as they go.

Where are you on the risk/reward continuum?

> **Action point:**
>
> What is your attitude to risk? Do you need to change your thinking in this area? If so, how exactly?

The Dream List

Imagine this: What's on your dream list? I don't mean your bucket list – that's not quite the same thing. I mean your list of lifetime pinnacle achievements. Things that will get you out in your stretch zone – playing for real in the place where you will make major leaps forward in confidence.

What are the key organisations you would like to work with? Who might be your 'blue chip' clients – the people that you aspire to work for above all others? Do you want to sell your work to a major retailer? Do you want to develop services for a global charity? Do you want your videos to be at the big national and international film festivals – or go viral online? Do you want your specialist software used on a space mission?

Only you will know what these aspirational goals are.

Unless you write those goals down, unless you begin thinking about how you might actually achieve them, you will simply end up muddling along. Having a dream list is a really powerful thing. It's no good having the list, however, if you don't then work at building the relationships you need to make it happen.

Often what stops us in life is much less to do with the quality of our work than with the quality of our courage and ambition.

We all need an irritant to keep us moving – the grain of sand in the oyster shell, so to speak. Sometimes our own conscience simply isn't enough. That's why we need the 'buddy' I referred to earlier and why it's so important to meet with them regularly to review your goals and make sure that you are actually making some progress. Choose someone who shares your values and who is on roughly the same journey as you – it can then be a truly reciprocal and trusting arrangement.

Why is this all so difficult? Psychologically speaking, we are actually hardwired to avoid danger, to stay in our comfort zone. The bit of your brain that is responsible for making sure that you stand up straight and that you avoid obstacles and that you continue breathing is hardwired to keep us out of danger.

That means every time we try to do something new, something challenging, that bit of our brain kicks in and says no, you don't want to be doing that, there is a risk involved in that – stay safe, stay within your comfort zone. This is the root of procrastination – and you have got to force yourself to break through that.

The Dream List – step by step

1. Make your 'dream list'.

2. Find someone to hold you accountable – someone you respect. Your 'buddy'.

3. Work your way through it step by step.

4. Find out who the gatekeepers are (influential people that can open doors for you) and build relationships with them – step by step.

5. Stay close to people who support what you are doing and radiate warmth and energy in your direction.

6. Stay away from those who drain you or seek to diminish your efforts.

7. Be prepared to do things that take you outside your comfort zone.

8. Remember – being successful requires that you have to overcome resistance and challenge yourself.

Worksheet - The Dream List

This is a great exercise to do alone, or with a partner or collaborator. Use the worksheet or get a big sheet of paper and some markers and just write down in bullet point form all of your lifetime 'pinnacle' goals.

Make the list – and good luck!

8 Finding Your Platform

How and where do you want to be seen and heard in the world?

Where and how do you want people to find you? Which of the many platforms for self-promotion that are available feel most natural to you?

Avoid the angst of feeling that you have to do everything. You don't. The pundits will say you need to be Facebooking twice a day and Tweeting five times and updating LinkedIn and, and, and...you don't. Find the places you can hang out to greatest effect and perform (whatever shape that takes) with the maximum of comfort and ease and squeeze what you can from those.

Resist the pressure from people who try to persuade you to do far too much.

Be sure that your shyness or lack of confidence doesn't become an excuse not to show up. For some people disappointment becomes more acceptable than the discomfort of getting out there. If you have a gift you must share it.

If you have ever caught yourself saying 'Oh, I'm so disappointed in myself, I failed to do this that or the other...' please tell me you have thought about why. This is something you need to feel your way into. And irrespective of how confident you are, or you become, you will need to feel your way into every new technique you use for self-promotion.

Showing up in a new way or in a new environment should begin with quiet observation, followed by the mindful dipping of a toe in the water.

As you progress with these experiments you will eventually find the platforms that suit your natural style and your values. You will get to feel at home and at ease much more quickly. The one proviso is that you cannot do this without getting into your stretch zone (and therefore feeling temporarily ill at ease) at some point.

Confidence comes from probing and testing and getting into the stretch zone until you feel OK out there – then you must continue to 'rinse and repeat' until you've got solid foundations upon which to build real progress.

Be a tiny bit brave on a regular basis – a few successes and failures will really help build your confidence. How does failure build confidence? It helps you clearly identify the things that don't work so that you can discount them quickly and move on.

This will help you, step by step, to overcome the fear of failure or embarrassment.

Experiment with the limits of your bravery – I knew a bloke who went into the post office once and asked for a pound of haddock – the post-mistress looked slightly startled, the bloke burst out laughing, and a bit of fear dissolved in that moment. Experiment - break out of your normal state now and again. Loosen up.

All of the most successful people I know (and I mean people who are successful on their own terms – millionaire or hermit) play in their stretch zone. Unless you get out in your stretch zone you don't know where you may be comfortable in the future. Fear is not a good reason to avoid the stretch zone.

The stretch zone is the place where you overcome the fear. And eventually what you do in the stretch zone morphs into your comfort zone. Then you will be ready for fresh adventures. There's no shortcut to confidence building. It has to be practised. There are big personal challenges – and pain barriers – to be broken through.

Embrace your anxieties. I always think that if I'm not nervous, I'm not doing it right. I'd rather listen to a wobbly but genuine presentation that's delivered from the heart than a smooth but shallow one.

It's about learning to manage and live with nerves rather than avoiding things because you think being acutely nervous is somehow synonymous with you not being confident. All good presenters (and performers) suffer from sweaty palms and a sense of dread a lot of the time. When I did a TED talk I was very nearly physically sick a couple of minutes before going onstage.

Confidence comes from having strategies to manage these situations, not from eradicating the unpleasantness associated with them.

For example, it only takes a few practice runs to familiarise yourself with the fears and physical sensations associated with standing in front of an audience. Any seasoned speaker or performer will tell you that this is something you become accustomed to – which in turn helps diminish the fear somewhat.

Acknowledge your 'inner expert'

In previous writing, I have always encouraged people to overcome their resistance to the idea that they might be considered an expert.

Most of us tend not to regard ourselves as experts – and maybe even shrug in a self-deprecating way when someone else makes a really complimentary comment about our work. The odd thing is that we can all easily identify an expert or two in our field – individuals who are simply much more experienced, talented or inspired than we regard ourselves to be.

Think about this. Who do experts look up to? They do exactly what we do – they too identify people that they feel are more experienced, talented or inspired than they are. And so it goes on.

There will always be people who know more than you, and people who know less than you. Aspire to learn from those with more knowledge, and pass on your learning to those with less – in truth, that's the primary role of an expert.

One of the questions I am asked most frequently is this – 'How can I raise my profile, establish my credibility, and become known more widely for what I do?'

Showcase: The things you've achieved in life and work – be proud of the experience you have and don't be afraid to share it with others.

Increase your visibility: Be seen, be known, have a reputation for being a specialist. Hiding away doesn't do anyone any good at all! Give up the reluctance to stick your head over the parapet. Who do you want to be known by? – And for what? Brand yourself as the person that people seek out for these things.

Share: Success stories, facts, figures and testimonials – tell the story of your life and work and broadcast this where you can.

Communicate: Do talks, workshops, public appearances, use publicity, demonstrations of your skills and knowledge, speak up at meetings. This doesn't need to be complex – people will be interested.

Explain: Techniques, materials, processes – how your product or service evolved. Customers love to talk about the things they buy, so the more you can tell them, the better.

Distil your knowledge down to 'bite size' chunks of information. People will respect you if you give small amounts of high quality information at any given time.

Be approachable: A true expert shares and communicates freely.

Properly applied, your expert knowledge can help you develop new working relationships, refresh your networks and contacts, and vastly improve your chances of getting exactly where you want to go.

Are You A Natural Born Thought Leader?

There are lots of different definitions of Thought Leadership out there.

One simple definition is that a thought leader notices and comments on ideas and themes that are of interest to their niche, and comments consistently over time in such a way as to develop an audience for themselves, their company or their brand.

It's about establishing a relationship with and delivering something of value to your clients and customers that aligns with your values. By doing this you go beyond selling a product or service and establish yourself as an expert in that field. This makes people think about you differently in significant ways.

They get to like your point of view and look out for the contributions you make.

One of the great things about Thought Leadership is you don't need to be well-known or famous in order to establish yourself. You can start in tiny ways and build this up over time.

What do you notice each day? What do you find yourself sharing on Facebook and Twitter? Is there a consistent theme to this? One component of thought leadership is the consistency of what you share.

How do you share?

Do you like sharing audio, video or narrative (articles and links to things that others have written)? Many thought leaders choose a specific form of sharing – podcasts, say, or videos on a YouTube channel. Or you can blend what you do so that it appeals to a wide range of learning styles – this can be quite a successful technique to build an audience quickly.

Do you create original material?

To become a top notch thought leader, you must work towards creating original material. The very best bloggers work on this principle, and don't just write about themselves or their own product/ or services. They have an opinion – or interview others and share a range of opinions around a topic.

People often say to me, 'why do you share so much – aren't you worried people will steal your ideas?' Hmmm... for me, it's a no-brainer; isn't sharing the currency of our humanity, of culture, of love?

9 Relationships and Networking

I'm going to stick my neck out and say this: If the thought of attending networking meetings fills you with dread, and you think that you can connect with the right people without attending them, then don't go. Simple. There's no law that says you must.

However, you can't survive without strong relationships and networks. So – sometimes you simply must go to a meeting, conference or dinner party. Then you must employ your best Ninja tactics to achieve the same ends.

Don't go anywhere without a plan. Go with an aim or, better still, a person you wish to connect with, in mind.

Build rapport

Remember that you are at your most interesting when you show interest in the person you are talking to.

Listen carefully to the people you meet. Ask intriguing questions.

If the purpose of your self-promotional activity is to establish trust and build strong relationships with others so that they want to engage your services, buy your products or collaborate on projects, then learning how to build rapport is key to making that happen.

Don't just ask them what they do, ask about their ambitions, or at the very least ask what they hope to get out of attending the event. If you click, great. If not, you will be remembered as a friendly, interesting person.

The nature of the questions you ask of another human being can profoundly affect the outcome of the conversation. 'What's your name?' 'Where do you come from?' and 'What do you do?' are fairly blunt instruments in the lexicon of relationship building. 'Why?' and 'How?' are much better building blocks to a question – they elicit a more elaborate answer.

If, in my role as coach, I asked you to describe your long-term goals, I'd expect to get a brief, well-edited answer. The question itself has built in limitations. If on the other hand, I asked this: 'If all obstacles were removed, where could you be in 3 years time?' I'd probably get a much more imaginative answer – one that would then serve to lead to a very interesting conversation. It's not just about using 'open' and 'closed' questions – although that helps.

It's about using questions that fire up a journey within someone else's imagination.

Rather than asking stock 'who', 'what', 'where', 'when'

questions, which can trigger a defensive response, try to use words in your dialogue that open up the more imaginative part of your conversational partner's thinking: 'How do you imagine that will turn out for you?' 'I'm intrigued by your ideas, tell me more.' 'I'm fascinated to know what you think about xyz.' 'Has that changed the way you approach things now?' 'How will you do things differently this year?' 'How will you know that has been successful for you?'

These are dynamic questions that are interesting to think about and answer. By phrasing your questions in an interesting way, you make the other person feel differently about how they answer them. It engenders true dialogue rather than simple social exchange.

Olde worlde tactics

What if you identify someone on a friend's list on Facebook or Twitter but you are wary of Direct Messaging them? You could ask to be introduced personally by the friend, or ask them to introduce you more formally on Linked In. That's the really cool thing about old fashioned etiquette – having someone to introduce you reinforces your credibility and will do much more to cement a really good relationship than any direct message can.

Or what if... you were to sit down and write them a personal letter on good quality notepaper, enclose something interesting and intriguing, stick a stamp on it and put it in the postbox?

Making Extraordinary Things Happen

We are all capable of making extraordinary things happen. Inevitably, whatever you choose to do, other people will be central to your success.

Be careful to look after the relationships that sustain you. Work with people in such a way that they come to love (or at least respect) you and the things that you do. Metaphorically speaking, you need to build yourself a fortress of goodwill.

Become a trusted friend, a person that can be relied upon.

I'm not a religious person - but I do believe in the principle of karma. If I was allowed just one rule it would be to treat others in the way I wish to be treated myself. It's no accident that all of the principal faiths in the world share this tenet. It's what makes the world go round.

Put good stuff out there, good stuff tends to come back, measure for measure.

Social media

Used strategically, social media offers a huge opportunity to find, connect to and communicate with key individuals pretty much anywhere on the planet. Used randomly, it will eat up time and distract you from getting on with the important work.

Whether you are starting from scratch or already have followers, I'd encourage you to pause for a moment and ask yourself a few questions about why you are engaging with social media in the first place.

If marketing is all about building relationships with people who will subsequently connect with your business in some meaningful way and then say 'yes' to your proposition, goods or services, how best can your social media activity serve that aim?

Join. Observe. Follow.

Social media should first be used for watching how others behave, finding out who others are connected to, and noting what works and doesn't work for those already operating in your niche. Then connect yourself. Be forensic about this. Use the search function on each platform to find people or organisations that matter to you. Follow them.

Watch how other people in your niche are using social media, and in particular what, how and where they share. On the basis of what you see working, test a few different types of post. Observe more, test more, and gauge reaction. Test differently – what works best for you? Refine your approach, test again.

Don't ask for likes and shares and RT's. These should be earned, not begged or paid for. Get followers legitimately – by simply following people you want to connect with and posting interesting stuff. Bring your expertise and thought leadership into play. Always link your posts to something – your website, blog or shop. Don't do direct selling. Entice people to follow your trail of breadcrumbs – preferably to a place they can spend time reading, watching or browsing.

The pros and cons of Public Speaking

It's a bit of a paradox, the fact that speaking in public is one of the highest-ranking human fears. Why? Because speaking in public also just happens to rank as one of the most powerful ways of promoting ourselves. That's very clear when you're part of an audience listening to - or better still, participating in - an inspiring presentation.

However it's a different kettle of fish when it's you having to stand at the front and deliver it.

If you can overcome the fear, it can do some pretty amazing things for you:

- It creates a huge increase in trust – people see the authentic you.
- It's a relationship building exercise – as long as what you do is interactive.
- It's communication, market research and selling rolled into one.
- You can engage all learning styles much more comprehensively.
- It creates empathy – it creates a chance for people to get to like you. Your story is a crucial part of that.
- It's a chance to demonstrate your products, skills and abilities - adult show and tell.

I once came across a roadside glassmaker just outside the ground of Bellapais Abbey in North Cyprus. The man on the stall had a crowd of astounded people watching him produce tiny, tiny fully formed glass elephants - without the aid of magnifying equipment – in just a few minutes. And as he made the elephants he told the story of himself ('I'm in the Guinness records book you know') and his work and his tiny rickety stall.

He nailed every single one of those bullet points with ease.

When you are quiet or introverted it can feel odd standing up talking about yourself with just a PowerPoint to shelter behind. So why not create opportunities to get out there and do your authentic show and tell?

Public speaking is the number one fear for most adults because we suffer from impostor syndrome – the nagging fear of being 'found out' – or worse still, being ridiculed in public. It's a tough threshold of anxiety to clamber over. Put your skills and your work between you and the audience – and interact – and it all suddenly gets easier.

Dipping your toe in the water.

As with most extremely difficult things, I strongly advise that you begin by spending time observing others who practice this craft well. Work out what aspects of their presentation really work to engage the audience. The process of observation will help you clarify just how much skill, knowledge and ability you already have and how much you will need to acquire and practice before stepping onto the stage yourself.

There are two things that I found significantly helpful in getting over the fear. One was to visit a speaking club. Just to listen. I soon realised that the room was full of a strange mix of show-offs, experts, stumbling ingénues and complete beginners. All were on different rungs of the ladder of competence. There are four stages to the ladder:

- Unconscious incompetence
  (we've not thought about it yet)
- Conscious incompetence
  (we realise there is a challenge to be faced but don't yet know how to tackle it)
- Conscious competence
  (we start to practice it)
- Unconscious competence
  (we can do it without thinking)

You can't get to position four without going through the first three. It helps to watch others as they move through the process and climb the ladder – it renders the process visible and helps you begin to see it as a manageable task.

The second turning point for me, which came much later, was to attend and later speak at Pecha Kucha events. A Pecha Kucha event typically comprises six or seven presentations, all 20 slides long, with 20 seconds allotted for each slide. It's a great way to see what makes a well-honed presentation (or not) and when you are ready it helps you get out there with your first short presentation. The other speakers are generally very welcoming, understanding – and just as anxious as you, in equal measure.

Don't die onstage

We all know instinctively that one of the best ways to raise our profile is to get out there, show up, and talk directly to our target audience. Not quite so simple to do, as most of us, professional speakers included, suffer from nerves.

I don't know many people – and that includes some really experienced speakers and presenters - who wouldn't admit to getting the collywobbles in the run up to an appearance. Indeed, most agree that some degree of nervousness is a pre-requisite if you are to engage properly with your audience.

We all feel anxious about this – but what is the true source of the fear? Fear of public humiliation or embarrassment? Fear of being exposed as a fake? Fear of losing the place, drying up or simply freezing – like the proverbial rabbit in the headlights? In truth we all will have our own personal viewpoint on this – which may well take in any, all or some of the above.

I find myself either presenting or being presented to on a regular basis, so I get to see both sides of this up close and personal.

Here are a few suggestions and observations that might make the whole thing easier, or at the very least, enable you to feel more prepared.

Being nervous is OK

Interestingly, nervous speakers are usually given the benefit of the doubt – empathy kicks in and the audience finds itself willing the speaker to succeed. Unprepared speakers, however, get what they deserve. As do speakers who go – on – much - too – long.

Don't write a script

If you need notes, use a series of index cards with key words on. There's a huge difference between delivering a compelling presentation about your work and making a speech. I sometime put reminders on my slides, in tiny letters that only I can see, reminding me to tell a particular story or give a specific example. Often the tiniest prompt is all you need, and you can then be much freer in the way you present.

Before the event

Sort out as much as you can before the event. Get directions, check the availability of parking, find out who will meet you and when. Go onto Google maps and work out your journey time, and make allowances for delays. Talk to the organiser and check that everything you need – laptop, projector, screen, extension leads and things like flipcharts and pads, will all be in the room when you arrive. This may sound a bit basic, but you need to remove as much worry and uncertainty from the process as you can. If you arrive relaxed, you'll have a head start.

Getting Set Up

If you are canny, you will have arranged to get into the room as early as possible. I like to get in early enough to have a good poke around – to check where sockets and light switches are, that everything has been supplied as requested, and to find out about housekeeping, fire alarms and exits, and where toilets are.

When I've got everything set up, and tested my presentation, I then like to sit in various positions around the room to get an idea of what people can see. Just to check that I'm not obscuring anything by standing in my chosen position or that I've accidentally set something up that's out of someone's sight line.

And get yourself a good supply of water - stay hydrated.

Mental preparation

Your body language will be giving away a lot about how you are feeling. If you are nervous or feeling unprepared, then position yourself beside the person who is introducing you and start to make eye contact with the group while you are waiting to go on.

Consciously relax the muscles in your face, and smile. Scan round the faces of the whole audience front to back and right to left and back – say a silent 'Hello' to all of them in your mind's eye, and keep your hands steady by your sides or behind your back. For some, a steadying hand on the podium works a treat – just don't accidentally look as if the building will fall down if you let go.

Stay calm and take your time. We all tend to deliver our lines at zillion miles per hour when we are nervous, so breathe slowly, and form each line in your head before you begin to say it.

You can almost take twice as long to say things as you feel comfortable with before anyone notices – time seems to speed up when the adrenalin flows (just think of the 'my life flashed before me' notion). The truth is whilst you notice this, others don't.

Use the 'lighthouse' technique

Every group you address, large or small, will always have people within it who nod and smile and give unspoken feedback. You can then find yourself addressing these people and accidentally ignoring the rest.

Make sure your eyes scan the horizon, like the beam of light from a lighthouse, taking in every face in the room. That way everyone will feel you are making contact, and you'll get a richer response as a result. Use inclusive gestures – open arms, or an open palm.

Believe – in yourself and what you are saying

It's imperative that you deliver with energy and conviction – if you want other people to find your message compelling and believable, you have to believe it yourself. Only 7% of how you come across is down to the words you use – 38% is tone of voice, and a massive 55% is body language – and these two will reveal any lack of conviction on your part.

That's where creative people have a head start. We genuinely love and are enthusiastic about our chosen craft, and that will shine through despite any nerves that might be showing.

Start well

I often find asking a few simple questions will get people focused quickly. A bit of participation like 'Hands up those of you who have... (Insert the question of your choice here)' warms the audience up and gets them associating personally with you and your content. Or introduce a quirky fact or dilemma relating to your specialism (Did you know that glass was a liquid? or who invented the zip fastener?) - something that you will resolve or explain later – add in a bit of suspense.

Show and tell

You can also gain an advantage in that any visual material you show people, either on screen or in the flesh will draw people's attention away from you. So your primary task can be to tell the story of the work.

Choosing the right images – the ones that really fire your enthusiasm; images of things you've really enjoyed working on - can make all the difference to how you feel about your talk.

Moderate pace and tone

There's nothing like a bit of feedback to boost your confidence and keep your energy going. One way of ensuring you get this is to keep your audience alert by changing the pace and tone of your voice. It's amazing how this alone can make the difference between a lively engaging experience and a truly dull one.

Speed up and slow down deliberately (subtly, mind) and alter your intonation. Apart from anything else, it keeps you energised too.

Finish Well

Plan to finish well. Finish with something that really floats your boat. You'll then transmit that enthusiasm over to your audience. Let them know that you've enjoyed their company – thank them for coming. And don't be coy – enjoy the applause.

I would encourage you to have a really good try. I know it's not to everyone's taste, but if you can master it, it'll literally change the way you approach things. In the end, however, public speaking is only one option of many.

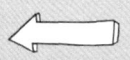

> **Action point:**
>
> If speaking to groups is not a strong point for you, where and when can you 'dip your toe in the water' by trying some of these things?

Destination Websites and Blogs

Is your website a destination, or a stopping off point on the way to your competitor's sites?

It's all very well getting people to visit your website - but what do they do when they get there - and how long do they stay? In some senses, the overall number of people who visit your site is relatively meaningless when taken in isolation.

You want your visitors to hang around, visit as many pages as possible, bookmark the page and come back again and again. So how can you persuade them to do that?

Ask yourself this question: What is it about a website or blog that makes you want to return? Certain sites can be relied on to provide a steady stream of new ideas and inspiration. Other sites solve problems or give a fresh slant on things. Some are just full of awesome visual content or informative video.

Create relationships, don't sell

If your blog or social media posts simply mimic your website sales page, why are you doing the same thing twice? Your posts should be about building a great relationship with your readers.

Online, this is a subtle process. You need to give your reader a reward for their visit – a bit of knowledge, something intriguing, inspiration, or the solution to a problem – something that leaves them wanting to come back for more. Here are some ways you can do that.

Generosity

The offer of free stuff used to simply be bait to capture your email address. But the web has changed - the giveaway has a social function now. The web is genuinely becoming a more sociable and generous space. Google has become less about keywords and title tags and more about quality of content, social sharing and quality of your storytelling. If you genuinely provide good content that people can interact with and share, you are also likely to show higher in the search engine rankings.

Google also rewards sites that offer downloadable content that links to playable or shareable media such as PDF files, video or podcasts.

So, to summarise, you must make your site more than just a shop window, gallery or shop. You must indulge in a bit of storytelling. And you must be both informative and generous with your content. This has a knock on effect in terms of perceived value too. The generosity of your communication will affect the way that people perceive the value in what you do, and therefore the price you can charge.

Don't forget that your visitors and customers all have different learning styles too. Some will prefer reading things, some looking at pictures and diagrams and some will be looking for content they can interact with.

How, exactly, can you make this work for you? How do you make something available to your customers (and potential new customers) without coming over as cheesy or desperate?

The trick to this is to tap into your natural expertise - what are you best at? What can you talk about and share with some authority?

How can you make this an interesting and valuable activity for both parties – you and the customer?

Whatever you do, don't shy away from this - if you are genuinely good at what you do, people will look up to you as an expert in your field. How can you capitalise on that effect to attract customers, build loyalty and keep them coming back?

One of the questions I regularly pose in my marketing sessions is this: What can you give away? Most people can usually identify one or two things that would work for them. Here are short descriptions of things you might like to try.

Product information sheets

A silversmith who specialised in top end gold and platinum wedding rings decided to create a detailed product sheet explaining how to clean and care for high quality jewellery.

Outstanding downloadable catalogues

If a customer is in a hurry, and you have a PDF download they can save and read later, they will often do so. A PDF can contain links, so it's easy for them to hop from the PDF straight back onto the website.

Advice

For example, useful information for customers on how to choose an appropriate gift with confidence – according to the age and gender of the recipient perhaps, or according to their budget.

'Show and Tell' videos

Video is a powerful tool – it is the single most powerful medium on the web. It's a great medium for storytelling, and means you can be found not only via your website but also via YouTube or Vimeo (or wherever you store your video)

I know one manufacturer who was amazingly successful with this. She created 'how to' videos and then upsold simple kits to make the exact item shown in the video. She now has her own online TV channel and sells globally.

Or you can simply document the way your business works – from raw idea through to the finished item. Write a little about your ideas, and the process or techniques you use. This will get you visits from both buyers and fellow business-owners.

Checklists and infographics

These relate closely to the 'how to' materials above, but some folk like to check things off on their journey – 10 steps to setting up a 'pop-up' shop, or how to prepare for a talk or masterclass, for example. These are great ways to share what you have learned and show off your expertise.

Quizzes

People love quizzes. They appeal to human beings' innate curiosity. One of the most re-tweeted things I've done – ever – was a creative business quiz.

Interview someone else

It's not all about you – or shouldn't be. Find someone whose work or opinion you find interesting, and go and interview them. Doing this live is best – you can be more spontaneous and take photos on the fly. Or, if travel is problematic, think up a list of questions and email them. Take their answers and a few photos that they have supplied and create your post. Link your article or post back to their website – then both of you share the link on your social media.

Review a trade fair or retailer

I'm often asked 'can you recommend a good trade fair to exhibit at?' Nightmare. What's heaven for one business can be hell for another. If you've been to a fair recently, write an honest review so that other businesses know what to expect, and put the link out on Facebook and Twitter. It'll get you some traffic.

Review a book

If you are a reader of books about small business, why not write reviews? Again, fellow traders want to know what the best books are. There are so many out there, money is tight, and it's hard to choose. Get reviewing. If you have an Amazon seller account, make a link through to the book on Amazon and make some money. Better still, contact the author and see if they'll give you an affiliate link – you could make around 30% on the sale that way.

Create a link to a useful resource

This is so easy – just do a web search on something topical - 'Pinterest for Business' or 'Opportunities for the self-employed' or 'Advice on pricing your work'. When you find an article that you feel hits the spot, write an introductory paragraph and share the link. A word of warning: don't try to re-write the piece and present it as your own – it's the research and sharing that's important.

Inspirational places

Write about inspirational places. Illustrate the article with photos and/or original drawings. Tell the story – what did you find inspiring, how did it fire up your emotions? How did it trigger your creativity? Tell people how to get there, recommend a campsite or B&B. Be an online tour guide. Travel writing was the birthplace of the blog – and it's still a topic well suited to the medium.

Solve a problem

Have you found a useful shortcut recently, or the solution to a technical problem? Or a new product that has really impressed you? Share the information. People love finding out about new stuff. Become the 'go to' person for solutions to tricky problems.

And finally:

Keep your content short, lively and to the point. Break up the written content with photos, video, and illustrations. Use sub headings to avoid big continuous chunks of text.

Developing Products

By extension, all of these things can be developed into products. We all dream of having something that will 'earn money while we sleep'. The logic goes like this.

First you create some free stuff to draw people to your site. When they have sampled the giveaway, offer them a low cost product (like an eBook) so that they can sample what you do in more depth (the low cost product needs to be really impressive). Then have a much higher ticket item that will be the real earner.

For example:

- A book or e-book
- An online course
- Live masterclasses
- Kits that can be given as gifts
- Impressive project plans that people follow step by step to create their own masterpiece. This works especially well with aspirational items: quilts for example, technically challenging items like furniture projects or working with precious metal clays. Some people really want to make great things but struggle to come up with the ideas and need help with the techniques by having them laid out step by step. The natural extension of this is to also provide the kits with all the materials part or fully prepared

Point to ponder:

What product, or products, might you wish to develop? How will they complement and support other work that you do? Quality content stimulates interest and encourages others to spread the word about what you do.

A final word on Quality.

Whatever you decide to do, your actions will only be sustainably successful if the following are true:

- **Quality** – everything you do is imbued with quality, and that needs to show on your site. No dodgy photos or home made graphics.
- **Track record** – you need to show that you can 'do what it says on the tin', and have some proof of that on your site – testimonials and quotes from happy customers.
- **Brilliant communication** – clear, crisp, simple words. Nothing wordy or pretentious. Everything to hand and easy to get at in a couple of clicks.
- **Confidence in what you do** – confidence shines through. Don't stick anything on your site unless you have a high level of confidence in it.
- **Open and friendly branding** – enable yourself to be loved by your customers.

And don't forget – the 'About Me' page is often the most visited page on small business websites. Tell your story well. Talk about yourself with confidence – but don't be boastful.

You are, by nature, one of the most fascinating people on the planet – you own and do things that others aspire to own or do themselves one day.

Exercise: Mapping out your expert profile

This exercise rounds off the way that you need to think about your choice of platform. Here's a way to figure out the right ways in which to comfortably package up your expertise.

Part One: A thought experiment

Think carefully about someone you admire, and whom you regard as being an expert in your niche. How do they behave – what are they doing in order to be seen and taken seriously? Here are a few prompts:

- Do they write a lot or keep a blog?
- Do they manage to get featured on websites and in magazines?
- Do they run classes?
- Do they appear at public events to talk and share skills?
- Do they have a YouTube channel?
- Do they host get-togethers to share ideas?
- Do they regularly collaborate with others?
- What else do they do that you like/enjoy?

List what they do – this is called 'modelling'. The idea is you find someone who behaves in the way that you would like to, and gets results from doing so. Then you can model your behaviour on theirs. N.B. This is not copying – it's simply a way of thinking about how you might put a variety of different approaches together.

Part Two: An exercise

Get a large sheet of paper and mind-map all the profile raising opportunities you can think of – see the 'starter' example here.

For example: if you are terrified of speaking in public, you may wish to avoid that and focus on mapping other promotional techniques.

As the layers of your mental picture build up, you will find yourself adding to this map – this is just a starting point. Jot down what you aspire to do. Don't worry if you don't yet know how you will make it happen – you will instinctively know when you are ready.

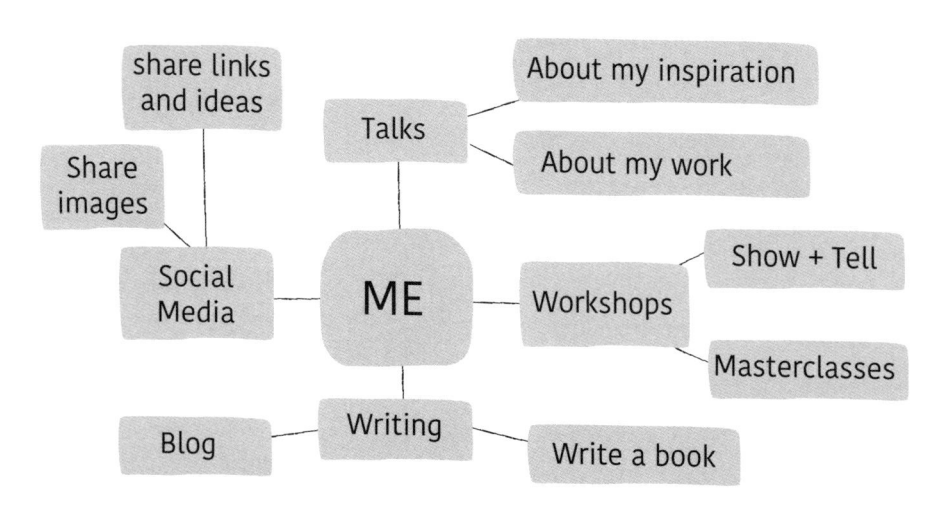

ME
- Talks
  - About my inspiration
  - About my work
- Workshops
  - Show + Tell
  - Masterclasses
- Writing
  - Blog
  - Write a book
- Social Media
  - share links and ideas
  - Share images

10 Asking for help is not an admission of failure.

This is a BIG issue for some people. Asking for help is not an admission of failure – on the contrary, it's an expression of courage, of integrity, of a willingness to embrace change, to learn and grow.

In fact, if you are not asking for help, you are under performing. Everyone needs help. Politicians, global entrepreneurs, no matter where on the spectrum, great people ask for help all the time.

Isolation can drag you down when you work alone. It's completely normal to run into situations where you don't know the answer, or become paralysed by seemingly conflicting options. Time to ask for help. And the process of finding help can have some really exciting spin-offs.

Our instincts tell us to beware of rejection, and yes, it's not a very pleasant experience. However, for every person that refuses to help you, there will be a couple who will willingly share their experience with you - and it's a rare situation where someone, somewhere, has not experienced and overcome precisely the problem you seem to be stuck with.

There are four or more potential outcomes from a request for help:

- An outright rejection - rare, but possible.
- A genuine attempt to help, or at least signpost you to someone more qualified.
- The beginning of a new and fruitful working relationship or networking opportunity.
- Serendipity puts you in exactly the right place to not only solve the problem, but change up a gear at the same time.

Years ago, I developed a creative workshop which I wanted to sell to schools. It worked, but only to a limited degree. Someone I met socially handed me the business card of a company in New York who specialised in running similar creative education workshops. One evening, whilst feeling a bit down, I wrote a letter to them, asking if they could recommend a solution to my problem.

A few days later, I got a call from the director. He invited me to go and work with them for three weeks - they would provide accommodation and advice, if I could raise the airfare. Needless to say, I jumped at the chance. I learned everything I needed to know at the time and gained a working relationship that lasted for years, with me returning to New York many times to work and visit my new friends.

The truth is, you never know when, where or how the next break will come, unless you remain open to opportunity and ask for help when you need it.

You must get used to saying what you want - out loud. You may be surprised by what happens as a result.

Who could help you most right now?

Radiators and drains

We all have 'radiators' - people who support us and exude warmth towards us - and 'drains' - people who, despite the best of their intentions, leave us feeling exhausted after each encounter.

Now and again, it pays to seek out a radiator and ask for a spot of support. It takes guts. It takes trust. There's always an element of risk. When it works, however, the payoff can be enormous.

By sharing the risk, by opening yourself to scrutiny, by asking for constructive criticism, the possibility of a positive outcome increases exponentially.

Working in isolation is hard enough - don't make it even harder on yourself by failing to spot the need for a bit of ruthless compassion from time to time. As often as not, you need it just at the point where the very idea horrifies you. Recognise the signs, overcome the resistance, and act accordingly.

Do you have a buddy you seek out when you need a bit of constructive criticism? How do you deal with troubled times?

Ruthless Compassion

I first came across the concept of ruthless compassion whilst studying for my coaching post-grad. Essentially, it describes an approach where one person is able to point out to another (hopefully in a timely manner) the need to rethink actions or behaviours in order to avoid a potentially damaging outcome.

It's the grown up equivalent of intervening when you see a child about to stick its finger in an electrical socket, or otherwise place herself in danger. You wouldn't just stand by and let disaster unfold, would you?

Once you grasp the value of the concept, it's easy to see that from time to time, it's worthwhile asking someone you trust to exercise ruthless compassion on your behalf. We all get a bit close to the edge sometime - tempted to launch an idea on the world without thinking it through; let something through our internal quality control without requisite scrutiny; respond to a difficult situation without taking time - or even recognising the need - to step back and count to ten before acting.

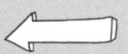

> **Action point:**
>
> Who do you know that would be good at helping you in this way?

The Personal 360

Don't rely on random opinion. Seek out structured feedback - a 360-degree view - of how you are doing now and again.

This widely used coaching exercise can be helpful in getting balanced feedback. You can use it exactly as it is, or adapt the questions. But be brave enough to ask questions that matter.

Choose a few people who know you really well, and a couple who know you, but are a bit more distanced from you. Explain that you need some honest feedback in relation to your professional and personal development. Ask if they would be willing to take part before you send the questions. And ask them to be honest.

Here's how to do it:

Ask them the following (or similar) questions:

- What is the first thing you think of when you think of me?
- What do you think is the most interesting thing about me?
- What one thing could I change for my own benefit?
- What do you think has been my greatest accomplishment?
- What do you value most about me?
- What do you perceive to be my greatest strength?

Be prepared for some surprises. Be open to new viewpoints. More often than not the answers will reveal interesting facets of yourself and your behaviour that you may previously have not appreciated. And you will probably get some very positive feedback about your strengths.

Working Collaboratively - strength in numbers

My work takes me out and about talking to creative people, business owners and public organisations. I'm really impressed by some of the things I've seen. Whenever times get tough, traditional funding streams shrink and get harder and harder to access.

A lot of people are troubled by the changes, and yes, the pace of ideologically driven change and the decimation of services as we have known them is quite sickening. However, it's the way we respond to situations that is the real measure of our collective mettle.

What's impressed me? Well, it's the degree of open minded, healthy, visionary collaboration. No whinging, no complaining. Just a clear view of what's required and a collective curiosity as to how to make it happen, with no need to follow old models or harp on about things being taken away.

This is the way forward. In the midst of all this change, the true survivors will be the ones who have:

- Taken responsibility for their own destiny.
- Sought out like minded people, collaborators or mentors.
- Taken the time to explore the nooks and crannies of possibility.
- Redrawn the Map.
- Taken some decisions, made some plans and – crucially:
- Started to act on them.

These are the people that will be taken seriously. Serial complainers fall by the wayside. Grumblers are passed over. I'm absolutely not saying we shouldn't protest. Just that protest and progress can only usefully coexist in the presence of smart thinking and action in both fields of endeavour. One mustn't be allowed to hold the other back.

If my job is to facilitate thinking, this is the way I want to work.

It has always been the case that people come together in testing times; part of that is the metaphorical huddling together for warmth, part is strength in numbers. However the extremely lengthy nature of this recession, coupled with uncertainty about the stability of the whole economic system has amplified that effect somewhat.

There's a big increase in partnership working right across the board – across government, across the private and public sectors, and within the creative industries - everyone wants to know who your 'partners' are.

Part of that is economic necessity - clustering operations and activities together to cut costs – but part of it is also driven by the recognition that there are many great things to be gained from working together as sole traders and small businesses. Necessity being the mother of invention, we're discovering all sorts of ways of making things happen in new, independently resourced ways.

It may not always seem obvious to an individual entrepreneur, perhaps working in isolation, that collaboration might just be the key that unlocks a more powerful and productive way of working. In truth, a lot of people are working collaboratively already without recognising they are doing it.

Collaboration can work for us on so many different levels - from working together to crowd-fund projects, through skill sharing and barter, to working with others to share messages and get things done via social media.

Solo entrepreneurs across the UK are collaborating to create pop-up shops, events and new services. More and more, creative people are getting together to do things that they previously relied on umbrella organisations or the local authority to arrange and fund.

From my own point of view, as a writer, mentor and speaker, the way that people engage with my services has changed radically over the last few years. The 'How much? – I'll apply for some funding for that' approach ceased suddenly, was followed by a huge drop in activity for a period and is now increasingly being replaced by 'How much? – I'll ask everyone to chip in and we'll make it happen'.

The world has stopped, de-fragmented, and re-booted with a fresh attitude. That attitude strikes me as incredibly healthy. People have stopped waiting for others to organise things and have realised that sometimes the only way to make things happen is to get things moving yourself.

Some people are still hanging around at the moment in the hope of getting a grant or waiting for funding to reappear. In most cases, it won't. Lateral action is what's required. If lots of people get together and chip in, it may even end up costing you less to do it yourself than if you pay the full rate to attend someone else's event.

Got an idea for an educational workshop? Don't wait for someone to ask you - it could take forever. Find a school near you and try it out. Is there a gap in the market for a local conference, fair or festival? Start one – the benefits will last much longer than the one-day event.

Need some specialist training? Get together with a group of like-minded people with similar requirements and organise the event yourself – the possibilities are only limited by the scope of your imagination.

An illustrator I mentored did very well from her Open Studio events each year, then had a brainwave to bring together a wildlife interpretation centre and a national wildlife charity and get them interested in hosting an exhibition of her work.

Each of the partners could see a benefit that worked for them, and the event that was created became of greater significance than the simple sum of the parts. It was a huge success, raised the profiles of the charity and interpretation centre and a lot of illustrations were sold.

A metalworker I coached was brilliant with metal, but when he partnered with a visual artist to create illustrative 2D designs that could be worked into ornamental ironwork, the ability to respond to commissions was enhanced by being able to offer a much broader palette of design options. It was a win-win partnership.

More and more, we are entering into partnership with people via social media – often in quite subliminal ways – liking, sharing, and recommending each other's work for example. We cross promote our products and services based on what we like and who is in our circle of fans and followers.

The folk who benefit most from this, of course, are the ones who notice activity, join the dots, write useful material based on what they see, and then share this for the benefit of the community. People pay attention and become interested in finding out more. The author of the shared material then benefits as a direct result of the initial generosity. This is thought leadership in a highly adapted form.

The new collaboration goes further, even. Online petitions and consultations cannot be ignored, are highly democratic in nature, and probably have a more direct and immediate effect than following the traditional route of lobbying and consultation.

Sole-traders and small businesses also benefit from this. Whole movements of collaboration and collective action are evolving and literally springing into action across the country. Art joins with food joins with complementary medicine joins with the energy of the people who have noticed – and chosen to do something about it rather than waiting. All it requires is to notice the relationships between things.

For example, local companies who do complementary rather than competing things notice the alignment of their business values and then figure out a way of working together for mutual benefit.

It's all about doing things differently, putting people and their values first and telling the right stories to engage customers, fans and followers.

11 Preparing for Action

Take time for yourself

My thoughts often turn to a topic that's close to many creative people's hearts – notably, finding the time to dream up new ideas. It's a subject that creates tensions for us all – creating and maintaining that fine balance between optimum creativity and a healthy bank balance.

We all suffer from 'cobbler's children' syndrome. It's a biblical theme of course, around spending so much time fulfilling everyone else's needs that we forget our own. That's dangerous when you run a business that is dependent on a continuous flow of new ideas and products. From a business advisor's point of view, we spend too much time working in the business – keeping up with demand - rather than on it, innovating and developing.

From a marketing specialist's point of view, that is a fatal error. A business without new products in development is not viable in the long term.

It is easy to see then that taking time out to innovate is really rather important. Not only is it desirable to take time out to dream up new products and experiment with new ways of working - it is essential to your businesses' long-term survival.

But – and it's a big but – it's really hard to do. Cash requirements snap at our heels, orders must be filled, the telephone must be answered. Urgent and important issues fill every nook and cranny of our waking lives. The paradox is this – just at the point when we're busiest creating and shipping one product, we really ought to be thinking of the next big thing. When it goes quiet it's too late to get the new products and the marketing going again for the next cycle. We can end up with an uncomfortable gap.

So, how do you make the time to dream? We all need time to dream, time to get in the creative flow. Often as not, it can't be done sitting at a desk, or at our workbench.

The familiarity of the space and the constant incoming demands just freeze us up. And if you do manage to create the time in your diary, procrastination or creative block kicks in. Have you noticed this? There's a little bit of psychology that's helpful in understanding what is happening here. Psychologists refer to the lizard brain – the amygdala – it's the bit of our brain that pays attention to basic stuff like breathing, heartbeat, and vital signs. It also keeps us out of trouble – it's the bit that creates the flight or fight response when danger looms.

But, funnily enough, as a side effect of the survival response, the lizard brain produces a resistance to change. Lizard says 'this is what we've always done – best just keep doing it this way'. It actively doesn't like us thinking about new ways to do things. So, effectively, creative block is hard wired into the system and we need to find ways to fool the brain into letting go, letting us be playful for a while.

Historically, lots of our major thinkers – artists, entrepreneurs and scientists alike – have realised that you need to actively disconnect from the notion of your work and your workspace in order to free up the creative mind.

Einstein used to go and lie in a cornfield in the sun. Steven Spielberg talked about dreaming for a living. When I'm coaching someone who is clearly locked up and can't think straight, never mind connect with their creativity, I usually suggest going out and wasting some time. It's counterintuitive, but it works.

What might be the thing that works for you? For me, (very much an Einstein fan) it can be a walk in the woods, or lying on my back on a grassy patch, or lolling in a deckchair on the lawn. Do I feel guilty? Yes. Does feeling guilty solve anything? No. Does a quiet space, steady breathing and the emptying out of distraction work? Oh yes!

The other curious thing, and I'm sure you've noticed this, is that the funny space you enter when you are really relaxed – just before you fall asleep, or just as you wake up, for example – is often the time when you have your best ideas. How many of you have to go and write an idea down when you wake up – or jump out of bed to do so, just as you were falling asleep. It's not an accident.

Back to the lizard brain. Just at the point of wakefulness, the barrier between our subconscious and conscious mind relaxes. The Lizard is off guard. The great ideas pop out. That's why dear old Albert went to lay down in the cornfield.

Give yourself some time to chill, and the ideas will start to pop out. Try to force it, and they'll stay stuck. Try it. The other thing that tends to get in the way of creativity – a lot, in my experience – is the pressure that money issues create.

The danger here of course is that you get into the habit of thinking so much about work, money and survival that higher level functioning around creativity, mastery and the love of what you do gets completely lost. And the loss of those things can stop inventive thinking in its tracks.

Without the ideas, the state of flow, the gaining of mastery through experimentation and practice, everything else grinds to a halt for lack of life-blood.

So – what are the implications of all this?

If a business without new products is a business without a future, it's clearly vital to get the time out in order to think about what happens next. If you are too busy filling orders to unleash your creativity, what has happened to the heart and soul of your business? What brought you here in the first place?

If taking time out creates the space to dream, to innovate, to slip a few ideas past the lizard brain, how can you possibly afford not to?

Sabbaticals and Retreats

Sometimes a couple of hours of 'time out' just aren't enough to get the job done. Often it is necessary to change gear completely, clear your mind and make space for new thinking. If that is what is required, then do whatever you need to do to get away and find that precious space. Easy enough, I hear you say, if you live alone and don't have others depending on you. I'm lucky and have an understanding partner. So every now and again I go away for 3 or 4 days when I need to get my head around a challenge.

If you are relied upon by others – or vice versa - you may need to pluck up courage to ask if it's OK to take time for yourself. Again, not easy I know. All I can say is that once you have got past the obstacles, the benefits of taking the time will far outweigh the effort involved.

Make sure you choose somewhere you can be free of distractions - a little hideaway somewhere – or find someone who's going away and who will let you house-sit for a few days. There's almost always a way.

Exercise - The Wheel of Self-Promotion

Wheels have been used as coaching tools and aids to constructive thinking for millennia. They date back to early Buddhist thinking – perhaps earlier. A Google image search for 'wheel of life' will find lots of very beautiful examples and some more modern derivations.

This variant is based on the notion that we need to have self-promotion skills in a number of key areas. If that balance is not there, we may not make the progress we would like to. This exercise reveals areas where we are more, or less satisfied with our efforts – and therefore gives us a golden opportunity to think what action is required to ensure a good spread of self-promotional activity.

The Wheel:

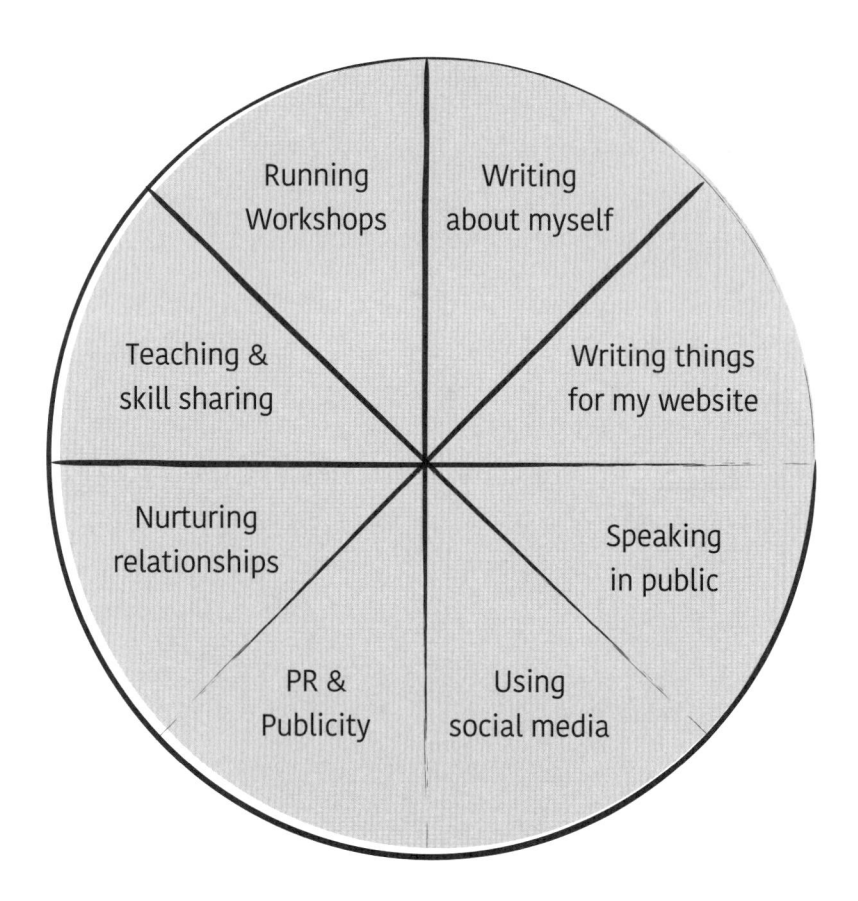

Wheel segments (clockwise from top-right): Writing about myself; Writing things for my website; Speaking in public; Using social media; PR & Publicity; Nurturing relationships; Teaching & skill sharing; Running Workshops.

How to do the exercise:

You can do this on your own, or pair up with a friend that you trust. Make a copy of the wheel diagram. Go round the wheel, scoring yourself for each segment instinctively on a scale of 1-10 where 10 = I do this well and 1 = I do this less well.

What is your current score in each area?

Go round again, identifying areas you'd like to work on – probably the areas where you scored lowest.

- Which areas would you most like to develop?
- How might you do that?
- What help or support might you need to move forwards?

I use this exercise regularly with my clients. Why? Because getting out there, building relationships and communicating with people about your work is the single most important thing you can do. There is no point in having a wonderful product or fabulous service if it's not visible in the world.

Even if you don't feel that anything is innately wrong with things as they are, these exercises are a useful touchstone. Used now and again, they can help you be aware of adjustments that it would be healthy for you to make.
Have a go. And if you can sit down with a trusted friend and look at the wheel together, you may be able to make suggestions and support each other in making useful progress.

12 What now?

Gather together all your notes and workings from the various exercises throughout the book.

Revisit this question first - it's the coaching question that I love most and use a lot: 'If all obstacles could be removed, where would you like to be in 3 years time? What are the obstacles, how can you remove them?'

It's a powerful exercise for two reasons – it forces us to think ahead and it asks us to think of what might be if there were no obstacles in our path.

The danger is that when we try to think too far into the future all our self-limiting beliefs kick in alongside all of the well-rehearsed reasons that we have for not making changes in our lives.

In truth, if we really want to make the change there are very few obstacles that cannot be removed or mitigated in some way. Think about the changes you want to make. How do you tend to move forward with things? Are you a 'one a day' person who likes to progress things in small steps – or are you an 'all or nothing' kind of person who likes to take massive action and get things done in one blast of energy?

Whatever you do, tell someone about your hopes and dreams. The act of sharing your intentions tends to lock you into taking action. At the end of every training session I run, I ask the participants to choose their main action point and say it out loud. I often get people emailing me later to say they have done it. It's almost as if they feel a sense of responsibility to me, having shared it publicly with the group.

> **Action point:**
>
> Share your hopes, dreams and ambitions with more people. You never know what resources the listener might have that they could bring to bear on your behalf. They may be the gatekeeper who has a key to a door that you had previously thought to be locked, barred or otherwise inaccessible.

Worksheet - The Future Timeline

Find your reverse timeline from page 74. The reverse timeline and the future timeline should marry up in the middle. The middle will always be here and now.

Use the future timeline to map out pinnacle goals, things from your dream list, practical and achievable interim milestones and the key actions and stopping off points along the way.

Be bold with this – map it out on a flipchart sheet or a long sheet of lining paper. Use colour, stick pictures on it, and use sticky notes if you think you might want to move things around.

Be playful. Above all be ambitious.

Be a little bolder, and shout a little louder each time you revisit it.

NOTES

FUTURE

NOW

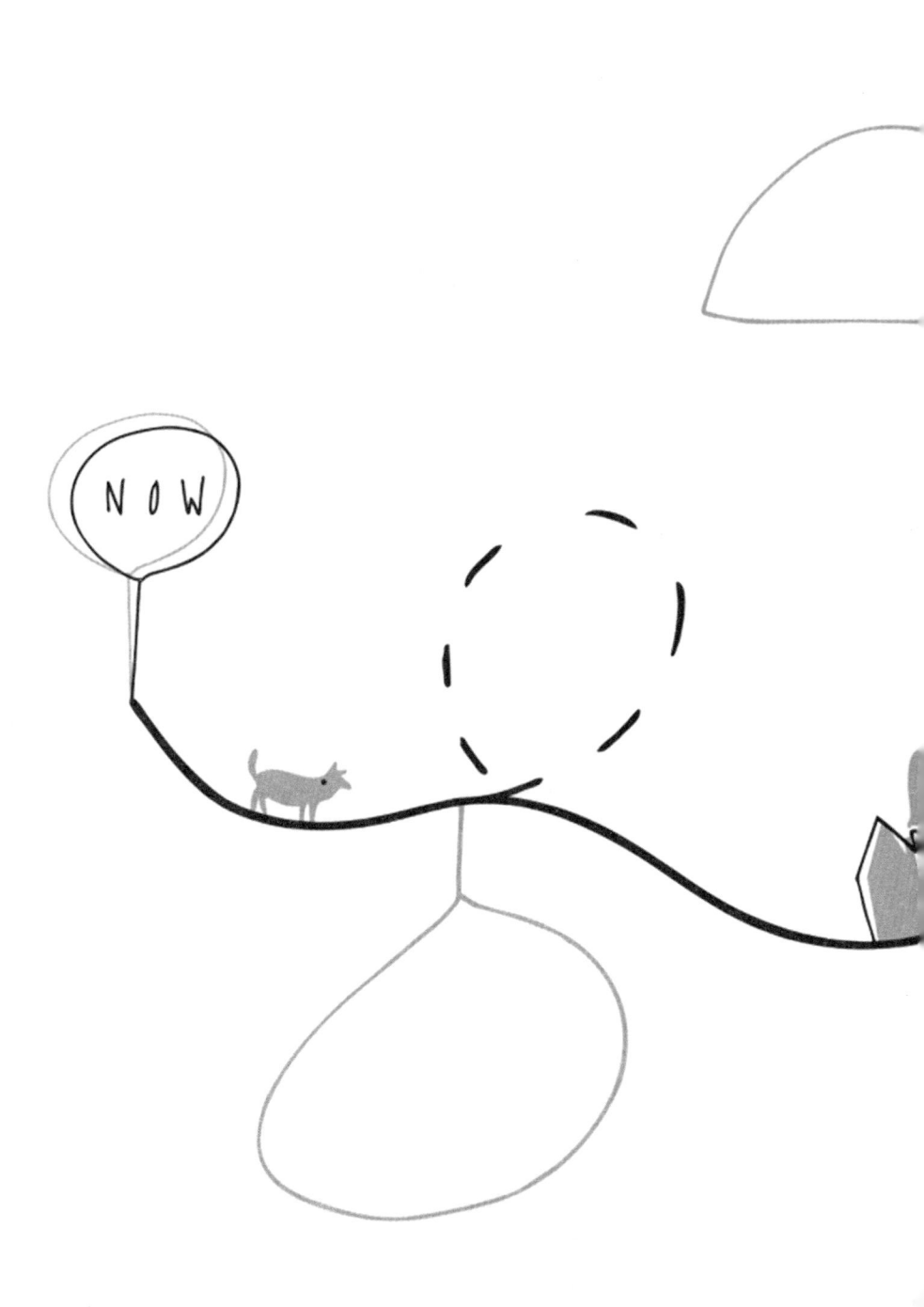

NOTES

Write A Cheeky Letter Today

I am a big advocate of boldness. I always encourage the people I work with to be bold, aim high, and write cheeky letters. What do I mean by cheeky? I guess I mean the sort of letters that stand out for their boldness, enthusiasm and desire to do what it takes to get on in life. Letters that are not shy of asking for help, targeted at those who are in the best place to provide a timely 'leg up'.

I'm a great fan of cheeky letters. Some of the best things I've ever done – and some of the most significant, have come about because I dared myself to write a cheeky letter.

Follow these rules:

Ask the right person: Do they have the power to help you?

Is the context right? Do they have the resources to help you with your idea?

Ask the right question: Have you thought this through – is your request relevant and complementary to their work and values?

Is your timing right? Is your request timely – will it fit with their calendar and workflow? Research this.

Ask the right way: Have you thought about the best way to approach them? How do you imagine they might like to be asked?

If you can say yes to all of these questions, then go for it.

What's the worst thing that can happen?

Remember that the process – working towards the goal, can be more important than the goal. The goal is an indicator of future performance. As you learn, the goalposts might move. Don't wait until you have defined your 'perfect' goal. You know that is a trap. Avoid the traps.

Above all – be yourself. That's the hardest thing on earth for someone else to copy.

Good luck, but above all, just do it!

Pete